WHO OWNS THE MOUNTAINS?

HENRY VAN DYKE

WHO OWNS THE MOUNTAINS?

HENRY VAN DYKE

*C*lassic Selections Celebrating
the Joys of Nature

EDITED AND INTRODUCED BY JAMES S. BELL, JR.
Compiled by Peter N. Shearn

NORTHFIELD PUBLISHING
CHICAGO

*In memory of Charles Clifford Bell,
a man of quiet but strong integrity;
and for the dim but pleasant memories
of fishing with him for catfish
in the Mississippi River*
J.S.B.

*To Barbara, my wife,
morning light and evening peace,
even if cloud or storm increase;
the blessing nature has surely shown,
you are the fairest of all I have known*
P.N.S.

THE FOOTPATH TO PEACE

To be glad of life because it gives you the chance to love and to work and to play and to look up at the stars;

to be contented with your possessions, but not satisfied with yourself until you have made the best of them;

to despise nothing in the world except falsehood and meanness and to fear nothing but cowardice;

to be governed by your admirations rather than by your disgusts;

to covet nothing that is your neighbor's except his kindness of heart and gentleness of manners;

to think seldom of your enemies, often of your friends, and every day of Christ;

and to spend as much time as you can, with body and with spirit, in God's out-of-doors

—these are little guideposts on the footpath to peace.

HENRY VAN DYKE

CONTENTS

BOOKS FROM WHICH
SELECTIONS WERE TAKEN

Books by Henry van Dyke:

Little Rivers. New York: Charles Scribner's Sons, 1895.
   A Handful of Heather
   At the Sign of the Balsam Bough
   Little Rivers
   Trout Fishing in the Traun

Fisherman's Luck. New York: Charles Scribner's Sons, 1899.
   Who Owns the Mountains?
   The Open Fire
   A Wild Strawberry

The Blue Flower. New York: Charles Scribner's Sons, 1902.
   The Source

Days Off. New York: Charles Scribner's Sons, 1907.
   Between the Lupin and the Laurel
   Among the Quantock Hills

The Poems of Henry van Dyke. New York: Charles Scribner's Sons, 1911.
   Ode: God of the Open Air

Camp Fires and Guide Posts. New York: Charles Scribner's Sons, 1921.
   Christmas Greens (Written in Autumn)

Book by Edwin Mims and Brooke van Dyke:

The van Dyke Book. New York: Charles Scribner's Sons, 1911.
   A Child's Point of View

INTRODUCTION

When the confines of our workplaces or homes become akin to the poet William Blake's "dark satanic mills," it is time to open the windows and experience the vast expanse of the open air. The elements the ancients spoke of—air, earth, fire, and water—both invigorate us and provide a serenity that the works of our hands cannot create. Rather, these timeless forces within the created order work their own enchantment upon us, broadening our vision, allowing us to be outside looking in, as it were, and viewing our place in the vast scheme of things—things of great beauty and wonder.

In *Who Owns the Mountains?* Henry van Dyke invites us to go on a grand excursion with him. He bids us sniff the pine-scented forests, feel the cool spray of rushing streams, be transfixed by the crackle and glow of the campfire, and be awed by the sublimity of mountain heights.

Along with the sensual intake of these elements, van Dyke is in no hurry to miss the denizens of each local habitat. Those dwellers of earth, air, and water

—the trees, rabbits, birds, and especially those venerable creatures, the fish—do not escape his keen-eyed descriptions.

The author is vaguely reminiscent of the fervent fly-fishing minister in the film *A River Runs Through It*. In addition to his dedication to that sport amidst the glories of nature, van Dyke too was a Protestant pastor. He graduated from Princeton Theological Seminary, was a Moderator in the General Assembly, and produced theological works. But he was also a national figure with a significant role in the politics of World War I. Short story writer, literary biographer, lecturer, essayist, naturalist, poet, hymn writer, Murray professor of English at Princeton University, and Ambassador to Luxembourg—his accomplishments in all these fields have been largely forgotten. Presently, he is noted for a Christian short story, *The Other Wise Man*; and I have recently edited his other tales of the Yuletide, now in print as *A Treasury of Christmas Stories*.

Seemingly hidden among these other lofty words of spirituality and literature is a cache of nature essays with such homespun titles as *Fisherman's Luck*, *Days Off*, *Little Rivers*, and *Camp Fires and Guide Posts*. A consummate outdoorsman, his passion for the four elements permeated his preaching, writing, and relationships. He took fishing and hunting expeditions throughout the U.S. and Canada, as well as Scotland, Norway, and New Zealand. As he pursued his literary and political callings, he also fished in Europe, Japan, and Palestine.

As a true lover of nature, van Dyke was also a good steward of resources. Beginning in 1883 he was a pioneer in preservation of the Adirondack region and took part in the conservation movement under President Roosevelt. He describes in a letter to a newspaper a process we know all too well today: "The once-lovely Racquette River, the fairest, wildest stream I ever floated on, . . . now changed into a dismal and desolate canal floating through the graveyards of a noble forest."

Faced with modernity and the Industrial Age, the Victorian and post-Victorian periods of van Dyke reacted with somewhat of an idealistic and romanticized view of nature. In his father's biography, his son Tertius speaks of him thus: "Never a specialist in any one field, his knowledge of fish, flowers, birds, trees, water and land, was often surprising. Even during the years when there were many literary nature fakers loose in the land he was never tempted by the obvious rewards to join their shoddy company."

It is the relaxed eye of the amateur naturalist and the skilled fisherman combined with the unforced poetic or spiritual insight that creates the right ambience in these selections. We are present with the author in a restorative mode, and without pedantry or contrivance on his part. We are served a quiet feast of simple fare, a bounty of nature's beauty and goodness. Our multiple senses delight in a field of laurels ablaze or a simple jack-in-the-pulpit flower. Some of these encounters may provoke powerful memories, nameless joys of the past. The author writes: "But there is a nameless valley among the hills where you can still trace every curve of the stream; and see the foambells floating on the pools below the bridge. . . . There is a small flower trembling on its stem in some hidden

11

nook beneath the open sky, that never withers throughout all the changing years. . . . It abides forever in your soul, an unfading word of beauty and truth."

Whether we trudge across the heather of Scotland, among the chestnuts of Quebec, or the purple cyclamen petals of Austria, in the solitude we feel strangely at home, at least temporarily. In the selection on his visit to England he sums up the purpose of his nature writings. Describing the local scene of two of his favorite lyrical nature poets, Wordsworth and Coleridge, he says, "It was a day and scene to calm and satisfy the heart."

In the solitude and repose of the "little river" and "craggy peak" we find beauty, yes, but also the shimmering outline of goodness and truth. There is a sense of longing for a communion that was lost. He states elsewhere that, though we are not a part of it, we are, in a sense, married to nature. We both give and receive. In his era of the modern world, factory smoke despoiled the pristine qualities of nature. In our post-modern present, we ourselves feel tainted and alienated, seeking the reunion described above.

Though someone may hold a title deed to a plot of land, we all own the mountains. We are very rich indeed, if only we'll claim our inheritance. It is my hope that in this little volume you, the reader, will discover a part of it.

JAMES S. BELL, JR.

A CHILD'S
POINT OF VIEW

My father, Henry van Dyke, was born in German-
town, Pennsylvania, on November 10, 1852. But when
he was very young the family moved to Brooklyn, and
it was there that most of his boyhood was spent. From
the first his relationship with his father was a particu-
larly beautiful one, for besides the natural trust and
reverence, there grew up the closest kind of friendship. It was as comrades that they went off for their
day's holiday, escaping from the city and its flag pave-
ments and brownstone fronts and getting out into the
fresh country air, to walk through the woods and
watch the leaves turn red and gold and brown and
drop to the ground or to skate in the winter or to
listen for the song of the first returning bluebird in
the spring. It was under the wise and tender guidance
of his father that my father's instinctive love of nature
grew and developed.

We were city children, but the woods were our
inheritance and fishing became our favorite sport.
Our earliest recollections of my father are in connection with fishing or camping expeditions. For when

work pressed too heavily and his health showed signs of too much wear and tear, he would take a few days in the spring and spend them catching the first trout of the season out of the Swiftwater, a little river in the Allegheny Mountains in Pennsylvania. When he was away we always thought that he had "gone fishing," and our earliest ambition was to go with him. Somehow, the fact that I was a girl never seemed to make any difference in my castles in the air, and all of us, boys and girls alike, grew up with the idea that to be like Father was the highest possible attainment.

As soon as we were able to read, we read his stories of camping that came out in the magazines. The article on "Ampersand" was the first and appeared in *Harper's Magazine* in 1885. But we were too young then, of course, to appreciate them, and I am afraid we preferred the story of "The Little Girl in the Well" and "Tommy Lizard and Frankie Frog" and other wonderful tales that he invented and told us between supper and bedtime.

Every Sunday we all sat in a row up in the second pew in the big church and heard him preach. Then in the afternoon, or on stormy Sundays, we put the chairs in the nursery in rows, and one of us would preach while the others were congregation or choir. This was the nearest we ever came to appreciating the sermons that were all the time being made down in the study just below us. During this time he published *The Reality of Religion, The Story of the Psalms, God and Little Children,* and *The Poetry of Tennyson,* besides many magazine articles. The sermons we liked best, though, were the Christmas sermons, which were always stories, and which were afterward published. Among them were "The Other Wise Man," "The Lost Word," and "The First Christmas Tree."

When we saw his books coming out we were fired with the ambition to publish books too, so we had a "Book Company," which he encouraged by his patronage. We wrote stories, laboriously printed them with pen and ink, illustrated them in watercolors, and bound them in cardboard and colored paper. We soon had quite a library, with contributions from all the family, and in all this my father was our wisest friend and critic. So the making of books was a reality to us, and we were interested not only in the writing, but in the illustrations and binding.

The best times of all, though, were the summer months when we left the hot, dusty city and went down to the little white cottage on the south shore of Long Island. Here he first taught us the gentle art of fishing, and how well I remember the morning he spent showing us how to catch the minnows for bait in a mosquito net (for catching the bait was always part of the game) and then how he stood with us for hours on the high drawbridge across the channel, showing us the easy little twitch of the wrist that hooks the fish and how to take him off the hook and save the bait. They were only young bluefish, or little "snappers," as we called them, and seldom more than eight inches long, but we were as proud as though they were salmon. Real trout we had never caught, though we had often jumped up from the supper table and run to meet him when he came in after dark with his basket full of wet, shiny, speckled ones. Then how exciting it was to weigh the biggest one and hear about the still bigger one that got away. That was always a good reason for going back the next day, and sometimes, if we had been very good, he would take one or two of us up under the bridge and up the narrow, winding stream, till we came to where the branches interlaced overhead and the boat would go no farther. There he left us at the little rustic bridge and waded up the stream above, while we sat breathless to hear his *halloo,* which meant he was coming back, and to find out what luck he had in those mysterious mazes above the bridge.

Those were the happiest days of our summer, and, as my father says, it was the stream that made them so.

But these were only day trips, and I longed for real camping out. Every fall my father went hundreds of miles away up to Canada where there were real bears and wolves in the woods and where you traveled for days without seeing a house or a person. I had often heard him tell his experiences much as they are now recorded in "Camping Out." Especially did we become interested in the French guides, whose letters to him I read eagerly, though slowly, for they were written in French.

Finally, to my earnest entreaties, there came a sort of half promise that I might go some time when I was bigger and stronger, but it seemed so indefinite that I quite despaired, and great was my surprise and joy one day when my father asked me if I would like to go camping that very day. The tent and the great heavy blankets and rubber sheets were taken out of their canvas wrapping where they were lying waiting for the fall and Canada. My father put on his corduroys and homespun and his old weather-stained gray felt hat, with the flies stuck all around the band, and I donned my oldest sailor suit, and with a few pots and pans, a small supply of provisions that the family helped us get together and our two fishing rods, we were ready for the start.

We took the long trip (about a mile) in an old flat-bottomed row boat, and my mother and little brothers came with us to see us settled. Our camping ground was in a pine grove near a small inlet to the saltwater bay on which our cottage faced so that, although the stream was blocked with weeds and stumps, the easiest way to get there was by water. We reached the place about four in the afternoon, moored the boat, and carried the tent and provisions up a little hill to the place my father had chosen. It seemed miles and miles from home and very wild. We had nothing for supper, and I remember wondering whether my father would shoot some wild animal or whether we would catch some fish. The latter course was chosen, much to my disappointment, and after the tent was pitched, the provisions unpacked, and my mother and brothers had left us all alone, we started out with rods and tackle to catch our supper.

Fortunately the fish were biting well, and with my rising appetite they came more and more frequently, until we had a basketful. Then we had to stop by the stream to prepare them for the pan, so it was almost dark when we threaded our way back through the deep forest of pines to the little white tent. But we soon built the fire and made things look more cheerful. How good the fish looked as they sizzled away over the glowing fire, and they tasted even better, eaten right out of the same pan they were cooked in. That was one of the best suppers I ever recall eating, and surely half the pleasure came from the comradeship of a father who shared and sympathized with my thoughts and entered into my fun with the spirits of a boy.

It was an experience I shall never forget, and, like most of the delightful "first" things I have done, I shall always associate it with my father. For he was our guide in everything; and besides the fishing trips, there were long Sunday afternoon walks through the woods and a growing acquaintance with the songs of the birds and with the wildflowers. He made us listen for the first notes of the bluebird in spring and to the "Sweet—sweet—sweet—very merry cheer" of the song sparrows that sang in the lilac hedge around our cottage. It was there that he wrote "The Song Sparrow" and a good many of the poems that came out later in a book called *The Builders and Other Poems.* But my first realization that my father was a poet came when my two brothers and myself were brought down to Princeton in 1896 to hear him read the ode at the one hundred and fiftieth anniversary of Princeton College.

In 1900 he was called to be the first occupant of the Murray chair of English Literature at Princeton University, and we now have, what we have always wanted, a home in the country. Here, though he has left the strain and rush of city life, he seems busier than ever, for he still preaches every Sunday, usually at university and college chapels, and his calendar is always filled with lecture engagements all over the country. Preacher, poet, lecturer—his professions are many, though his aim is one, to lift the world up and make it a better, happier one than he found it.

About three summers ago there were so many stories on this waiting list that my father knew they would give him no peace of mind until written down in black and white. We were spending that summer on an island off the coast of Massachusetts, and our little cottage was in the midst of all the merrymaking, near the ocean, and facing a field where all sizes of boys played baseball every afternoon. It was not at all an atmosphere for writing, so my father, on one of his walks of discovery to the middle of the island, found an old deserted farmhouse standing back from the road on a little rise of ground. There were apple trees around it and a grape vine straggling over the trellised porch, and from the window of what once was probably the sitting room there was a tiny glimpse of the blue sea far away in the distance.

No discordant sounds reached this quiet spot, and here my father spent a good part of the summer writing a great many of the stories in *The Blue Flower*. He would go out to his farmhouse study every morning, returning in body, though not in spirit, to lunch, and then go out again to work for the rest of the afternoon. As soon as a story was finished, we would gather, after supper, around the lamp, and he would read it to us. What a delight it was to recognize some of our old friends or familiar places, or to make the acquaintance of new and even better ones. We were sorry when the stories were all finished and the book had gone to the publisher.

But in spite of his many duties he still finds time to fish, and since we have lived here he has taken me on a real camping trip in Canada and taught me to catch real salmon, as well as showing me the scenes of a good many of his stories in *The Ruling Passion*. So now I know what real fisherman's luck is, for though "we sometimes caught plenty and sometimes few, we never came back without a good catch of happiness," and my father has taught me the real meaning of the last stanza of "the Angler's Reveille":

> Then come, my friend, forget your foes and leave your
> fears behind,
> And wander out to try your luck with cheerful, quiet
> mind;
> For be your fortune great or small, you'll take what
> God may give,
> And through the day your heart shall say,
> *'Tis luck enough to live.*

Brooke van Dyke
Avalon, Princeton, N.J.
January 21, 1905

PART 1

BRAVING THE ELEMENTS
(EARTH, AIR, WATER, AND FIRE)

CHAPTER 1

WHO OWNS
THE MOUNTAINS?

My heart is fixed firm and stable in the belief that
ultimately the sunshine and the summer, the flowers
and the azure sky, shall become, as it were, interwoven into man's existence. He shall take from all their
beauty and enjoy their glory.

RICHARD JEFFERIES, *The Life of the Fields*

It was the little boy who asked the question; and the
answer also, as you will see, was mainly his.

We had been keeping Sunday afternoon together
in our favorite fashion, following that pleasant text
that tells us to "behold the fowls of the air." There is
no command of Scripture less burdensome to accept
or more profitable to obey than this easy out-of-doors
commandment. For several hours we walked in the
way of this precept, through the untangled woods
that lie behind the Forest Hills Lodge, where a pair of
pigeon hawks had their nest; and around the brambly
shores of the small pond, where Maryland yellow-
throats and song sparrows were settled; and under the
lofty hemlocks of the fragment of forest across the
road, where rare warblers flitted silently among the

treetops. The light beneath the evergreens was growing dim as we came out from their shadow into the widespread glow of the sunset on the edge of a grassy hill, overlooking the long valley of the Gale River and uplooking to the Franconia Mountains.

It was the benediction hour. The placid air of the day shed a new tranquillity over the consoling landscape. The heart of nature seemed to take a repose more perfect than that of common days. A hermit thrush, far up the vale, sang his vesper hymn, while the swallows, seeking their evening meal, circled above the river fields without effort, twittering softly now and then, as if they must give thanks. Slight and indefinable touches in the scene, perhaps the mere absence of the tiny human figures passing along the road or laboring in the distant meadows, perhaps the blue curls of smoke rising lazily from the farmhouse chimneys or the family groups sitting under the maple trees before the door, spread a sabbath atmosphere over the world.

Then said the young boy, lying on the grass beside me, "Father, who owns the mountains?"

I happened to have heard, the day before, of two or three lumber companies that had bought some of the woodland slopes; so I told him their names, adding that there were probably a good many different owners, whose claims taken all together would cover the whole Franconia range of hills.

"Well," answered the boy, after a moment of silence, "I don't see what difference that makes. Everybody can look at them."

They lay stretched out before us in the level sunlight, the sharp peaks outlined against the sky, the vast ridges of forest sinking smoothly toward the valleys, the deep hollows gathering purple shadows in their bosoms and the little foothills standing out in rounded promontories of brighter green from the darker mass behind them.

Far to the east, the long comb of Twin Mountain extended itself back into the untrodden wilderness. Mount Garfield lifted a clear-cut pyramid through the translucent air. The huge bulk of Lafayette ascended majestically in front of us, crowned with a rosy diadem of rocks. Eagle Cliff and Bald Mountain stretched their line of scalloped peaks across the entrance to the Notch. Beyond that shadowy vale, the swelling summits of Cannon Mountain rolled away to meet the tumbling waves of Kinsman, dominated by one loftier crested billow that seemed almost ready to curl and break out of green silence into snowy foam. Far down the sleeping Landaff Valley the undulating dome of Moosilauke trembled in the distant blue.

They were all ours, from crested cliff to wood base. The solemn groves of firs and spruces, the plumed sierras of lofty pines, the stately pillared forests of birch and beech, the wild ravines, the quivering thickets of silvery poplar, the far peaks with their wide outlooks, and the cool vales resounding with the ceaseless song of little rivers—we knew and loved them all; they ministered peace and joy to us; they were all ours, though we held no title deed and our ownership had never been recorded.

What is property, after all? The law says there are two kinds: real and personal. But it seems to me that the only real property is that which is truly personal, that which we take into our inner life and

make our own forever, by understanding and admiration and sympathy and love. This is the only kind of
possession that is worth anything.

A gallery of great paintings adorns the house of
the Honorable Midas Bond, and every year he adds a
new treasure to his collection. He knows how much
they cost him, and he keeps track of the quotations at
the auction sales, congratulating himself as the price
of the works of his well-chosen artists rises in the
scale and the value of his art treasures is enhanced.
But why should he call them his? He is only their
custodian. He keeps them well varnished and framed
in gilt. But he never passes through those gilded frames
into the world of beauty that lies behind the painted
canvas. He knows nothing of those lovely places from
which the artist's soul and hand have drawn their inspiration. They are closed and barred to him. He has
bought the pictures, but he cannot buy the key. The
poor art student who wanders through his gallery, lingering with awe and love before the masterpieces, truly
owns them far more than Midas does.

Pomposus Silverman purchased a rich library a
few years ago. The books were rare and costly. That
was the reason Pomposus bought them. He was proud
to feel that he was the possessor of literary treasures
that were not to be found in the houses of his wealthi-
est acquaintances. But the threadbare Bücherfreund,
who was employed at a slender salary to catalog the
library and take care of it, became the real proprietor.
Pomposus paid for the books, but Bücherfreund enjoyed them.

I do not mean to say that the possession of much
money is always a barrier to real wealth of mind and

heart. Nor would I maintain that all the poor of this world are rich in faith and heirs of the kingdom. But some of them are. And if some of the rich of this world (through the grace of Him with whom all things are possible) are also modest in their tastes and gentle in their hearts and open in their minds and ready to be pleased with unbought pleasures, they simply share in the best things that are provided for all.

I do not speak of the strife that men wage over the definition and the laws of property. Doubtless there is much here that needs to be set right. There are men and women in the world who are denied the right to earn a living, so poor that they perish for lack of daily bread, so full of misery that there is no room for the tiniest seed of joy in their lives. This is the lingering shame of civilization. Someday, perhaps, we shall find the way to banish it. Someday, every man shall have his role in a share of the world's great work and the world's resulting joy.

But in the meantime it is certain that, where there are a hundred poor bodies who suffer from physical deprivation, there are a thousand poor souls who suffer from spiritual poverty. To relieve this greater suffering, there is no need to change the laws, only change the heart.

What does it profit a man to be the landed proprietor of countless acres unless he can reap the harvest of delight that blooms from every root of God's earth for the seeing eye and the loving spirit? And who can reap that harvest so completely that there shall not be an abundant gleaning left over for all mankind? The most that a wide principality can yield to its legal owner is a living. But the real owner can gather from a field of goldenrod, shining in the August sunlight, an unearned bounty of delight.

We measure success by accumulation. The measure is false. The true measure is appreciation. He who loves most has most.

How foolishly we train ourselves for the work of life! We give our most arduous and eager efforts to the cultivation of those faculties that will serve us in the competitions of the marketplace. But if we were wise, we should care infinitely more for the unfolding of those inward, secret, spiritual powers by which alone we can become the owners of anything that is worth having. Surely God is the great proprietor. Yet all His works He has given away. He holds no title deeds. The one thing that is His is the perfect understanding, the perfect joy, the perfect love of all things that He has made. To a share in this high ownership He welcomes all who are poor in spirit. This is the inheritance of the saints in light.

"Come, my boy," I said, "let us go home. You and I are very rich. We own the mountains. But we can never sell them, and we don't want to."

CHAPTER 2

A WILD
STRAWBERRY

The Swiftwater Brook was laughing softly to itself as it ran through a strip of hemlock forest on the edge of the Woodlings' farm. Among the evergreen branches overhead the brightly dressed warblers—little friends of the forest—were flitting to and fro, twittering their June songs of contented love: milder, lazier notes than those in which they voiced the romantic raptures of May. Prince's Pine and golden loosestrife and pink laurel and blue harebells and purple-fringed orchids and a score of lovely flowers were all abloom. The late spring had hindered some; the sudden heats of early summer had hastened others; and now they seemed to come out all together, as if nature had suddenly tilted up her cornucopia and poured forth her treasures in spendthrift joy.

I lay on a mossy bank at the foot of a tree after a frugal lunch thinking how hard it would be to find in any quarter of the globe a place more fair and fragrant than this hidden vale among the Allegheny Mountains. The perfume of the flowers of the forest is more sweet and subtle than the heavy scent of tropical blossoms. No lily field in Bermuda could give a fragrance half so magical as the fairylike odor of these woodland slopes, soft carpeted with the green of glossy vines above.

Nor are there any birds in Africa, or India, more exquisite in color than these miniature warblers proudly showing their gold and green, orange and black, and blue and white against the dark background of the rhododendron thicket.

But how seldom we put a cup of pleasure to our lips without a dash of bitters, a touch of faultfinding. My drop of discontent that day was the thought that the northern woodland, at least in June, yielded no fruit to match its beauty and its fragrance.

There is good browsing among the leaves of the wood and the grasses of the meadow, as every well-instructed angler knows. The bright emerald tips that break from the hemlock and the balsamlike verdant flames have a pleasant savor to the tongue. The leaves of the sassafras are full of spice, and the bark of the black birch twigs holds a fine cordial. Crinkle-root is spicy, but you must partake of it delicately, or it will bite your tongue. Spearmint and peppermint never lose their charm for the palate that still remembers the delights of youth. Wild sorrel has an agreeable, sour, shivery flavor.

But, after all, these are only appetizers. They whet the appetite more than they appease it. There should be something to eat in the June woods as satisfying to our sense of sight and hearing and smell. Blueberries are good, but they are far away in July. Blackberries are luscious when they are fully ripe, but that will not be until August. Then the fishing will be over, and the angler's hour will be past. The one thing that is lacking now beside this mountain stream is some fruit more luscious than grows in the tropics, to melt upon the lips and fill the mouth with sweetness.

But that is what these cold northern woods will not offer. They are too reserved, lofty, and austere to make provision for food and drink. They are not friendly to luxury.

As I shifted my head to find a softer pillow of moss after this philosophic review, nature gave me her silent answer. Three wild strawberries, nodding on their long stems, hung over my face. It was an invitation to taste and enjoy their goodness.

The berries were not the round and rosy ones of the meadow, but the long, slender, dark crimson ones of the forest. No more than three on that vine; but each one as it touched my lips was a drop of nectar and a crumb of ambrosia, a concentrated essence of all the pungent sweetness of the wildwood, palatable, penetrating, and delicious. I tasted the odor of a hundred blossoms and the green shimmering of innumerable leaves and the sparkle of the sifted sunbeams and the breath of highland breezes and the song of many birds and the murmur of flowing streams—all in a wild strawberry.

In *The Compleat Angler*, Izaak Walton quotes from a certain "Doctor Boteler" about strawberries. "Doubtless," said that wise old man, "God could have made a better berry, but doubtless God never did."

Well, the wild strawberry is one that God made.

I think it would have been pleasant to know a man who could sum up his reflections upon the important question of strawberries in the same fashion as that which Walton repeats. His tongue must have been in close communication with his heart. He must have had a fair sense of the ability to enjoy God's created order without which Christian piety itself is often dull and otherworldly.

I have often tried to find out more about him, and someday I hope I shall. But up to the present, all that the books have told me of this obscure sage is that his name was William Butler and that he was an eminent physician, sometimes called "the Esculapius of his age who was the Roman god of medicine." He was born at Ipwich in 1535 and educated at Clare Hall, Cambridge, in the neighborhood of which town he appears to have spent most of his life in high repute as a practitioner of medicine. He had the honor of doctoring King James the First after an accident on the hunting field and must have proved himself a pleasant old fellow, for the king looked him up at Cambridge the next year and spent an hour in his lodgings. This wise physician also invented a medicinal beverage called "Doctor Butler's Ale." I do not quite like the sound of it, but perhaps it was better than its name. This much is sure, at all events: either it was really a harmless drink, or else the doctor must have confined its use entirely to his patients; for he lived to the ripe age of eighty-three years.

Between the time when William Butler first needed the services of a physician in 1535 and the time when he last prescribed for a patient in 1618, there was plenty of trouble in England. Bloody Queen Mary sat on the throne, and there were all kinds of quarrels about religion and politics; and Catholics and Protestants were killing one another in the name of God. After that the red-haired Elizabeth, called the Virgin Queen, wore the crown and waged triumphant war and tempestuous love. Then Fat James of Scotland was made king of Great Britain; and Guy Fawkes tried to blow him up with gunpowder and failed; and the king tried to blow out all the pipes in England with his *Counterblast Against Tobacco*; but he failed too. Somewhere about that time, early in the seventeenth century, a very small event happened. A new berry was brought over from Virginia—*Fragraria Virginiana*—and then, amid wars and rumors of war, Doctor Butler's happiness was secure. That new berry was so much richer and sweeter and more generous than the familiar *Fragraria vesca* of Europe that it attracted the sincere interest of all persons of good taste. It inaugurated a new era in the history of the strawberry. The long lost masterpiece of Paradise was restored to its true place in the affections of man.

Is there not a touch of lighthearted contempt for all the vain conflicts of humanity in the grateful statement with which the old doctor greeted that comforting gift of Providence?

"From this time forward," he seems to say, "the fates cannot bother me, for I have eaten strawberries. With every Maytime that visits this distracted island, the white blossoms with hearts of gold will arrive. In every June the red drops of pleasant savor will hang among the scalloped leaves. The children of this world may scuffle and give one another wounds that even my good ale cannot cure. Nevertheless, the earth as God created it is a fair dwelling and full of comfort for all who have a quiet mind and a thankful heart.

Doubtless God might have made a better world, but doubtless this is the world He made for us; and in it He planted the strawberry."

Fine old doctor! Brave philosopher of cheerfulness! The Virginian berry should have been brought to England sooner, or you should have lived longer, at least to a hundred years, so that you might have welcomed a score of strawberry seasons with gratitude and wise sayings.

Since that time a great change has passed over the fruit that Doctor Butler praised so well. That product of creative art that Divine wisdom did not choose to surpass, human industry has labored to improve. It has grown immensely in size and substance. The traveler from America who steams into Cork Harbor in early summer is presented (for consideration) with a cabbage leaf full of pale-hued berries, sweet and juicy, any one of which would outbulk a dozen of those that used to grow in Virginia when Pocahontas was smitten with the charms of Captain John Smith. They are superb, those light-tinted Irish strawberries. And there are wonderful new varieties developed in the gardens of New Jersey and Rhode Island, which compare with the ancient berries of the woods and meadows as Leviathan with a minnow. The huge crimson cushions hang among the plants so thick that they seem like bunches of fruit with a few leaves attached for decoration. You can satisfy your hunger in such a berry patch in ten minutes, while out in the field you must pick for half an hour, and in the forest three times as long, before you can fill a small tin cup full.

Yet, after all, it is questionable whether men have really bettered God's masterpiece in the berry line. They have enlarged it and made it more plentiful and more predictable in its harvest. But sweeter, more fragrant, more poignant in its flavor? No. The wild berry still stands first in its subtle gusto.

No other high-titled fruit that ever took first prize at an agricultural fair is half so delicate and satisfying as the wild strawberry that dropped into my mouth under the hemlock tree beside the Swiftwater.

The trim plantations of trees that are called "forests" in certain parts of Europe—scientifically pruned and tended, counted every year by uniformed foresters, and defended against all possible violations—are admirable and useful in their way. But they lack the mystical enchantment of the fragments of native woodland that linger among the Adirondacks and the White Mountains or the vast, shaggy, sylvan wildernesses that hide the lakes and rivers of Canada. These Laurentain Hills lie in No Man's Land. Here you do not need to keep to the path, for there is none. You may make your own trail, wheresoever fancy leads you; and at night you may pitch your tent under any tree that looks friendly and firm.

Here, if anywhere, you shall dream of river and tree fairies. And if you chance to see one, by moonlight, combing her long hair beside the glimmering waterfall, or slipping silently, with gleaming shoulders, through the grove of silver birches, you may call her by the name that pleases you best. She is your discovery.

One side of our nature, no doubt, finds its satisfaction in the regular, the proper, the conventional.

But there is another side of nature, underneath, that takes delight in the strange, the free, the spontaneous. We like to discover what we call a law of nature and make our calculations about it and harness the force that lies behind it for our own purposes. But we taste a different kind of joy when an event occurs that nobody has foreseen or counted on. It seems like evidence that there is something in the world that is alive and mysterious and touched.

No array of personal accomplishments can rival the charm of an unsuspected gift of nature and goodness brought suddenly to light. I once heard a peasant girl singing down the Traunthal, and the echo of her song outlives, in the hearing of my heart, all memories of the grand opera.

The harvest of the gardens and the orchards, the results of prudent planting and patient cultivation, is full of satisfaction. We anticipate it in due season, and when it comes we fill our mouths and are grateful. But I pray, kind Providence, let me slip over the fence out of the garden now and then to shake a nut tree that grows untended in the wood. Give me liberty to put off my black coat for a day and go fishing on a free stream and find by chance a wild strawberry.

CHAPTER 3

LITTLE
RIVERS

There's no music like a little river's. It plays the same tune (and that's the favorite) over and over again, and yet does not weary of it like men fiddlers. It takes the mind out of doors; and though we should be grateful for good houses, there is, after all, no house like God's out-of-doors. And lastly, sir, it quiets a man down like saying his prayers.

ROBERT LOUIS STEVENSON, *Prince Otto*

A river is the most human and companionable of all inanimate things. It has a life, a character, a voice of its own and is as full of good fellowship as a sugar maple is of sap. It can talk in various tones, loud or low, and of many subjects, grave and light. Under favorable circumstances it will even make a shift to sing, not in a fashion that can be reduced to notes and set down in black and white on a sheet of paper, but in a vague, refreshing manner, and to a wandering air that goes "Over the hills and far away."

For real company and friendship, there is nothing outside of the animal kingdom that is comparable to a river.

I will admit that a very good case can be made out in favor of some other objects of natural affection. For example, a fair apology has been offered by those ambitious persons who have fallen in love with the sea. The sea is too large and too formless to love. It will not fit into our thoughts. It has no personality because it has so many. It is a salty abstraction. You might as well think of loving a glittering generality like "the American woman."

Mountains are more satisfying than the sea. It is possible to feel a very strong attachment for a certain range whose outline has grown familiar to our eyes, or a clear peak that has looked down, day after day, upon our joys and sorrows, moderating our passions with its own serenity. We come back from our travels, and the sight of such a well-known mountain is like meeting an old friend unchanged. But it is a one-sided affection. The mountain is voiceless and immovable; and its very loftiness and stateliness sometimes make us all the more lonely.

Trees seem to come closer to our life. They are often rooted in our richest feelings, and our sweetest memories, like birds, build nests in their branches. I remember the last time that I saw James Russell Lowell (only a few weeks before his musical voice was hushed); he walked out with me into the quiet garden at Elmwood to say good-bye. There was a great horse-chestnut tree beside the house, towering above the gable and covered with blossoms from base to summit—a pyramid of green supporting a thousand smaller pyramids of white. The poet looked up at it with his gray, pain-furrowed face and laid his trembling hand upon the trunk. "I planted the nut," said he, "from which this tree grew. And my father was with me and showed me how to plant it."

Yes, there is a good deal to be said in behalf of tree admiration; and when I recline with my friend Tityrus beneath the shade of his favorite oak, I consent to his devotions. But when I invite him with me to share my appreciation or wander alone to indulge the luxury of grateful, effortless thought, my feet turn not to a tree but to the bank of a river, for there the musings of solitude find a friendly accompaniment, and human relations are purified and sweetened by the flowing, murmuring water. It is by a river that I would choose to fall in love and to revive old friendships and to play with the children and to confess my faults and to escape from vain, selfish desires and to cleanse my mind from all the false and foolish things that mar the joy and peace of living. Like David's deer, I pant for the water brooks and would follow the advice of Seneca, who says, "Where a spring rises, or a river flows, there should we build altars and offer sacrifices."

The personality of a river is not to be found in its water nor its bed nor in its shore. Either of these elements by itself would be nothing. Confine the fluid contents of the noblest stream in a walled channel of stone, and it ceases to be a stream; it becomes what Charles Lamb calls "a mockery of a river . . . a wretched conduit." But take away the water from the most beautiful riverbanks, and what is left? An ugly road with none to travel it; a long, ghastly scar on the surface of the earth.

The life of a river, like that of a human being, consists in the union of soul and body, the water and the banks. They belong together. They act and react upon each other. The stream molds and makes the shore—hollowing out a bay here and building a long point there, alluring the little bushes close to its side and bending the tall slim trees over its current, sweeping a rocky ledge clean of everything but moss and sending a still lagoon full of white arrowheads and rosy knotweed far back into the meadow. The shore guides and controls the stream, now detaining and now advancing it, now bending it in a hundred sinuous curves, and now speeding it straight as a wild bee on its homeward flight; here hiding the water in a deep cleft overhung with green branches and there spreading it out, like a mirror framed in daisies, to reflect the sky and the clouds, sometimes breaking it with sudden turns and unexpected falls into a foam of musical laughter, sometimes soothing it into a sleepy motion like the flow of a dream.

And is it any different with the men and women we know and like? Does not the spirit influence the form and the form affect the spirit? Can we divide and separate them in our affections?

The stream and its channels are one life, and I cannot think of the swift, brown flood of the Batiscan River without its shadowy primeval forests, of the crystalline current of the Boquet without its beds of pebbles and golden sand and grassy banks embroidered with flowers.

Every country has its own special kind of river; and every river has its own quality. It takes insight and diligence to know and love as many as you can, seeing in each the fairest qualities and receiving from each the greatest enjoyment that it has to give. The torrents of Norway leap down from their mountain homes with plentiful waterfalls and run brief but glorious races to the sea. The streams of England move smoothly through green fields and beside ancient, sleepy towns. The Scotch rivers brawl through the open moorland and flash along steep Highland glens. The rivers of the Alps are born in icy caves, from which they gush with furious turbid waters. When their anger has been forgotten in the slumber of some blue lake, they flow down more softly to see the vineyards of France and Italy, the gray castles of Germany, and the verdant meadows of Holland. The mighty rivers of the West roll their yellow floods through broad valleys or plunge down dark canyons. The rivers of the South creep under dim tree-lined archways heavy with banners of waving moss. The Delaware and the Hudson and the Connecticut are the children of the Catskills and the Adirondacks and the White Mountains, cradled among the forests of spruce and hemlock, playing through a wild woodland youth, gathering strength from numberless tributaries to bear their great burdens of lumber and turn the wheels of many mills, originating from the hills to water a thousand farms, and descending at last, beside new cities, to the ancient sea.

Every river that flows is good and has something worthy to be loved. But those that we love most are always the ones that we have known best—the stream that ran before our father's door, the current on which we sailed our first boat or cast our first fly, the brook on whose banks we first picked the flower of young love. However far we may travel, we come back to Naaman's state of mind, speaking of his own rivers:

"Are not Abana and Pharpar, rivers of Damascus, better than all the waters of Israel?"

It is the same with rivers as it is with people: the greatest are not always the most agreeable, nor the best to live with. "I confess," says the poet Cowley,

> I love Littleness almost in all things. A little conven-
> ient Estate, a little cheerful House, a little Company,
> and a very little Feast, and if I were ever to fall in
> Love again, (which is a great Passion, and therefore, I
> hope, I have done with it,) it would be, I think, with
> Prettiness, rather than with Majestical Beauty.

I am all for little rivers. Let those who will chant in heroic verse the renown of Amazon and Mississippi and Niagara, but my prose shall flow in praise of the smaller rivers that are my favorite: Beaverkill and Neversink and Swiftwater, of Saranac and Racquette and Ausable, of Allegash and Aroostook and Moose River. Whenever I take my walks abroad it shall be to trace the clear Rauma from its rise on the field to its rest in the fjord or to follow the Ericht and the Halla-dale through the heather. The Ziller and the Salzach shall be my guides through the Tyrol; the Roth and the Dove shall lead me into the heart of England. My sacrificial flames of evening campfires shall be kindled with birch bark along the wooded stillwaters of the Penobscot and the Peribonea, and my cool drinks drawn from the pure current of Ristigouche and the Ampersand, and my altar of remembrance shall rise upon the rocks beside the falls Seboomok.

I will set my affections upon rivers that are not too great for intimacy. And if by chance any of these little ones have also become famous, like the Tweed

42

and the Thames and the Arno, I at least will praise them, because they are still at heart little rivers.

If an open fire is, as Charles Dudley Warner says, the eye of a room, then surely a little river may be called the mouth, the most expressive feature, of a landscape. It animates and enlivens the whole scene. Even a railway journey becomes tolerable when the track follows the course of a running stream.

What charming glimpses you catch from the window as the train winds along the valley of the French Broad from Asheville or climbs the southern Catskills beside the Esopus. Here is a mill with its dripping, lazy wheel, the symbol of quiet industry; and there is a white cascade, foaming in silent movement as the train clatters by; and here is a long, still pool with the cows standing knee-deep in the water and swinging their tails in calm indifference to the passing world; and there is a lone fisherman sitting upon a rock, rapt in contemplation of his rod. For a moment you become a partner in his tranquil enterprise. You turn around, you crane your neck to get the last sight of his motionless profile. You do not know what kind of fish he expects to catch or what species of bait he is using, but at least you pray that he may have a bite before the train swings around the next curve. And if by chance your wish is granted and you see him expertly draw some unknown, reluctant, shining reward of patience from the water, you feel like swinging your hat from the window and crying out, "Good work!"

Little rivers seem to have that indefinable quality that belongs to attractive people in the world—the power of drawing attention without courting it, the faculty of exciting interest by their very presence and way of doing things.

The most fascinating part of a city or town is that through which the water flows. Idlers always choose a bridge for their place of meditation when they can find it; and, failing that, you will find them sitting on the edge of a pier or embankment, with their feet hanging over the water. You do not know London until you have seen it from the Thames. And you will miss the charm of Cambridge unless you take a little boat and go drifting on the placid Cam, beneath the bending trees, along the banks of the colleges.

But the real way to know a little river is not to glance at it in the midst of a hasty journey. You must go to its native haunts and see it in its youth and freedom; you must accommodate yourself to its pace and influence and follow its meanderings wheresoever they may lead you.

You may go as a walker, taking the riverside path or making a way for yourself through the tangled thickets or across the open meadows. You may go as a sailor, launching your light canoe on the swift current and committing yourself for a period of time to the delightful uncertainties of a voyage through the forest. You may go as a wader, stepping into the stream and going down with it, through rapids and shallows and deeper pools. Of these three ways I do not know which is best. But in all of them the essential thing is that you must be willing and glad to be led; you must take the little river for your guide, philosopher, and friend.

And what good guidance it gives you. How cheerfully it lures you on into the secrets of field and wood and makes you acquainted with the birds and the flowers. The stream can show you better than any other teacher how nature works her enchantments with color and music.

Go out to the Beaverkill River and follow its brimming waters through the budding forest to that corner we call the Painter's Camp. See how the banks are all enameled with the pale hepatica, the painted trillium, and the delicate pink-veined spring beauty. A little later in the year, when the ferns are uncurling their long fronds, the troops of blue and white violets will come dancing down to the edge of the stream and creep venturously out to the very end of that long, moss-covered log in the water. Before these have vanished, the yellow crowfoot and the cinquefoil will appear, followed by the star grass and the loosestrife and the golden Saint-John's-wort. Then the unseen painter begins to mix the royal color on his palette, and the red of the bee balm catches your eye. If you are lucky, you may find, in midsummer, a slender fragrant spike of the purple-fringed orchid. Yellow returns in the drooping flowers of the jewelweed, and blue repeats itself in the trembling harebells, and scarlet is glorified in the flaming robe of the cardinal flower. Later still, the summer closes in a splendor of bloom, with gentians and asters and goldenrod.

You never get so close to the birds as when you are wading quietly down a little river, casting your fly deftly under the branches for the wary trout, but ever on the lookout for all the various pleasant things that nature has to bless you. Here you shall come upon the catbird at her morning bath and hear her sing in a clump of pussy willows that low, tender, confidential song that she keeps for the hours of domestic intimacy. The spotted sandpiper will run along the stones before you, bowing and teetering in the friendliest manner as if to show you the way to the best pools. In the thick branches of the hemlocks that stretch across the stream, the tiny warblers, dressed in a hundred colors, chirp and twitter confidingly above your head; and the Maryland yellowthroat, flitting through the bushes like a little gleam of sunlight calls as well. Persistent note, never ceasing, even in the noonday silence, comes from the wood-pewee, drooping upon the bough of some high tree.

When the stream turns out into a clearing or down through the pasture, you find other and livelier birds: the robin, with his sharp, saucy call and breathless, merry warble; the bluebird, with his notes of pure gladness, and the oriole, with his wild, flexible whistle; the song sparrow, perched on his favorite limb of a young maple, close beside the water, and singing happily through sunshine and through rain. This is the true bird of the brook, after all, the winged spirit of cheerfulness and contentment, the patron saint of little rivers, the fisherman's friend. He seems to enter into your sport with his good cheer and for an hour at a time, while you are trying every fly in your book, from a black gnat to a white miller, to entice the crafty old trout at the foot of the meadow pool, the song sparrow, close above you, will be chanting patience and encouragement. And when at last success crowns your attempts and the many-colored prize is glittering in your net, the bird on the bough breaks out in an ecstasy of congratulation.

There are other birds that seem to have a very different temper. The blue jay sits high up in the withered pine tree, bobbing up and down and calling to his mate in a tone of affected sweetness, but when you come in sight he flies away with a harsh cry. The kingfisher, ruffling his crest in solitary pride on the end of a dead branch, darts down the stream at your approach, winding up his reel angrily as if he despised you for interrupting his fishing. And the catbird, that sang so charmingly while she thought herself unobserved, now tries to scare you away by screaming loudly.

As evening draws near and the light beneath the trees grows yellower and the air is full of filmy insects out for their last dance, the voice of the little river becomes louder and more distinct. The true poets have often noticed this apparent increase in the sound of flowing waters at nightfall. Gray, in one of his letters, speaks of "hearing the murmur of many waters not audible in the daytime." Wordsworth repeats the same thought almost in the same words: "A soft and lulling sound is heard/ Of streams inaudible by day." And Tennyson, in the valley of Cauteretz, tells of the river "Deepening his voice with deepening of the night."

It is in this mystical hour that you will hear the most celestial and entrancing of all birdnotes, the songs of the thrushes—the hermit and the wood thrush. Sometimes, but not often, you will see the singers. I remember once, at the close of a beautiful day's fishing on the Swiftwater, I came out just after sunset into a little open space in an elbow of the stream. It was still early spring, and the leaves were tiny. On the top of a small sumac, not thirty feet away from me, sat a veery thrush. I could see the pointed spots on his breast, the swelling of his white throat, and the sparkle of his eyes as he poured his whole heart into a long chant, the clear notes rising and falling, echoing and interlacing in endless curves of sound. Other bird songs can be translated into words, but not this. There is no interpretation. It is music as Sidney Lanier defines it: "Love in search of a word."

But it is not only to the life of birds and flowers that the little rivers introduce you. They lead you often into familiarity with human nature in undress, rejoicing in the liberty of old clothes, or of none at all.

A stream that flows through a country of upland farms will show you what is common in many paintings. Here is the laundry pool at the foot of the kitchen garden, and the tubs are set upon a few planks close to the water, and the farmer's daughters, with bare arms and gowns tucked up, are wringing out the clothes.

And what a pleasant thing it is to see a little country lad riding one of the plow horses to water, thumping his naked heels against the ribs of his steed. Or perhaps it is a riotous company of boys that have come down to the old swimming hole and are now splashing and gamboling through the water like a drove of white seals very much sunburned.

Perhaps you will overtake another fisherman on the stream. It may be one of those fabulous countrymen, with long cedar poles and bed-cord lines, who are commonly reported to catch such enormous strings of fish but who rarely, so far as my observation goes, do anything more than fill their pockets with minnows.

The trained angler, who uses the finest tackle and drops his fly on the water as accurately as Henry James places a word in a story, is the man who takes the most and the largest fish in the long run. Perhaps the fisherman ahead of you is such a one—a man you have known in town as a lawyer or a doctor, a merchant or a preacher, going about his business in the respectability of a business suit. How good it is to see him now in the freedom of a flannel shirt and a broad-brimmed gray hat with flies stuck around the band.

In Professor John Wilson's *Essays Critical and Imaginative,* there is a brilliant description of a bishop fishing, which I am sure is neither imaginative nor critical.

> Thus a bishop, sans wig and petticoat, in a hairy cap, black jacket, corduroy breeches and leathern leggins, creel on back and rod in hand, sallying from his palace, impatient to reach a famous salmon-cast ere the sun leave his cloud, . . . appears not only a pillar of his church, but of his kind, and in such a costume is manifestly on the high road to Canterbury and the Kingdom-Come.

I have had the good luck to see quite a number of bishops.

Men's "private diversions" are usually more interesting, and often more instructive than their formal manners in public. When they are off guard, they frequently behave better than when they are on parade. I get more pleasure out of Boswell's *Johnson* than I do out of *Rasselas* or *The Rambler.* The *Little Flowers of St. Francis* appear to me far more precious than the most learned German and French analyses of his character. There is a passage in Jonathan Edward's *Personal*

Narrative about a certain walk that he took in the fields near his father's house and the blossoming of the flowers in the spring, which I would not exchange for the whole of his dissertation *On the Freedom of the Will*. And the very best thing of Charles Darwin's that I know is a bit from a letter to his wife: "At last I fell asleep," he says, "on the grass, and awoke with a chorus of birds singing around me, and squirrels running up the tree, and some woodpeckers laughing; and it was as pleasant and rural a scene as ever I saw; and I did not care one penny how any of the birds or beasts had been formed."

Little rivers have small responsibilities. They are not expected to bear huge navies on their breast or supply a hundred thousand horsepower to the factories of a large town. Neither do you come to them hoping to draw out Leviathan with a hook. It is good enough if they run a harmless, amiable course and keep the groves and fields green and fresh along their banks and offer a happy alternate of nimble rapids and quiet pools.

When you set out to explore one of these minor streams in your canoe, you have no intention of newsmaking discoveries or thrilling and world-famous adventures. You float placidly down the long stillwaters and make your way patiently through the tangle of fallen trees and carry your boat around the larger ones with no loftier ambition than to reach a good campground before dark and to pass the intervening hours pleasantly "without offense to God or man." It is an agreeable and advantageous frame of mind for one who has done his fair share of work in the world and is not inclined to grumble at his wages.

It is not required of every man and woman to be, or to do, something great; most of us must content ourselves with taking small parts in the chorus, as far as possible without discord. Shall we have no little lyrics because Homer and Dante have written epics? Even those who have greatness thrust upon them will do well to lay the burden down now and then and congratulate themselves that they are not altogether answerable for the conduct of the universe. "I reckon," said a cowboy to me one day, as we were riding through the Badlands of Dakota, "there's someone bigger than me running this outfit. He can 'tend to it well enough while I smoke my pipe after the round-up."

There is such a thing as taking ourselves and the world too seriously, or at any rate too anxiously. Half of the secular unrest and dismal sadness of modern society comes from the vain idea that every man is bound to be a critic of life and to let no day pass without finding some fault with the general order of things or projecting some plan for its improvement. And the other half comes from the greedy notion that a man's life does consist, after all, in the abundance of the things that he possesses and that it is somehow or other more respectable and pious to be always at work making a larger living than it is to lie on your back in the green pastures and beside the still waters and thank God that you are alive.

And so I wish that your winter fire may burn clear and bright while you read these pages and that the summer days may be fair and the fish may rise willingly to your hook whenever you follow one of these little rivers.

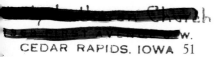

51

CHAPTER 4

THE
OPEN FIRE

It is a vulgar notion that a fire is only for heat. A chief value of it is, however, to look at. And it is never twice the same.

CHARLES DUDLEY WARNER, *Backlog Studies*

Lighting Up

Humans are creatures who have made friends with the open fire. All the other creatures, in their natural state, are afraid of it. They look upon it with wonder and dismay. It fascinates them, at times, with its glittering eyes in the night. The squirrels and the hares come pattering softly toward it through the underbrush around the camp. The fascinated deer stares into the blaze of the jacklight while the hunter's canoe creeps through the lily pads. But the attraction that masters them is one of dread, not of love. It is the witchcraft of the serpent's beguiling look. When they know what it means when the heat of the fire touches them, or even when its smell comes clearly to their most delicate sense, they recognize it as their enemy—the Wild Huntsman whose red hounds can follow for days without wearying, growing stronger and more furious with every turn of the chase. Let but a trail of smoke drift down the wind across the forest, and all the game for miles will register the signal for fear and flight.

Many of the animals have learned how to make houses for themselves. The hut of the beaver is a wonder of neatness and comfort, much preferable to the wigwam of his Indian hunter. The muskrat knows how thick and high to build the dome of his waterside cottage in order to protect himself against the frost of the coming winter and the floods of the following spring. The woodchuck's house has two or three doors; and the squirrel's dwelling is provided with a good bed and a convenient storehouse for nuts and acorns. The sportive otters have a toboggan slide in front of their residence; and the moose in winter make a "yard," where they can take exercise comfortably and find shelter for sleep. But there is one thing lacking in all these various dwellings—a fireplace.

Humans are the only creatures that dare to light a fire and to live with it because they alone have learned how to put it out.

It is true that two of his humbler friends have been converted to fire worship. The dog and the cat, being half-humanized, have begun to love the fire. I suppose that a cat seldom comes so near to feeling a true sense of affection as when she has finished her saucer of bread and milk and stretched herself luxuriously underneath the kitchen stove. As for a dog, I am sure that his admiring love for his master is never greater than when they come in together from the hunt, wet and tired, and the man gathers a pile of wood in front of the tent, touches it with a tiny magic wand, and suddenly the clear, consoling flame springs up, saying cheerfully, "Here we are, at home in the forest; come into the warmth; rest, and eat, and sleep." When the weary, shivering dog sees this miracle, he knows that his master is a great man and a lord of things.

A furnace is an underground prison for a toiling slave. A stove is a cage for a tame bird. Even a broad hearthstone and a pair of glittering andirons—the best ornaments in a room—must be accepted as an imitation of the real thing. The truly open fire is built in the great expanse, with the whole earth for a fireplace and the sky for a chimney.

To start a fire in the open is by no means as easy as it looks. It is one of those simple tricks that everyone thinks he can perform until he tries it.

To do it without trying—accidentally and unwillingly—is a thing for which any ignorant person is fit. You knock out the ashes from your pipe on a fallen log; you toss the end of a match into a patch of grass, green on top, but dry as punk underneath; you scatter the dead brands of an old fire among the moss —and a blaze is under way before you know it.

A fire in the woods is one thing—a comfort and a joy. Fire in the woods is another thing—a terror, uncontrollable fury, a burning shame.

But the lighting up of a proper fire—kindly, approachable, and serviceable—is a work of intelligence and skill. If, perhaps, you have to do it in the rain, with a single match, it requires no little art and skill. There is plenty of wood everywhere, but not a bit to burn. The fallen trees are waterlogged. The dead leaves are damp, the charred sticks that you find in an old fireplace area absolutely incombustible. Do not trust the handful of withered twigs and branches that you gather from the spruce trees. They seem dry, but they are little better for your purpose than so much asbestos. You make a pile of them in some apparently suitable hollow and lay a few larger sticks on top. Then you hastily scratch your solitary match on the seat of your trousers and thrust it into the pile of twigs. What happens? The wind whirls around in your little hollow, and the blue flame of the sulphur spurts and sputters for an instant and then goes out. Or perhaps there is a moment of stillness; the match flares up bravely; the nearest twigs catch fire, crackling and sparkling; you hurriedly lay on more sticks; but the fire deliberately dodges them, creeps to the corner of the pile where the twigs are fewest and dampest, snaps feebly a few times, and expires in smoke. Now where are you? How far is it to the nearest match?

If you are wise, you will always make your fire before you light it. Time is never saved by doing a thing badly.

The Campfire

In the making of fires there is as much difference as in the building of houses. Everything depends on the purpose that you have in view. There is the campfire and the cooking fire and the smudge fire and the little friendship fire—not to speak of other minor varieties. Each of these has its own proper style of architecture, and to mix them is poor art and use of resources.

The object of the campfire is to give heat—and light secondarily—to your tent or shanty. You can hardly build this kind of a fire unless you have a good ax and know how to chop. For the first thing that you need is a solid backlog, the thicker the better, to hold the heat and reflect it into the tent. This log must not be too dry, or it will burn out quickly. Neither must it be too damp, else it will smolder and discourage the fire. The best wood for it is the body of a yellow birch or, next to that, a green balsam. It should be five or six feet long, and at least two and a half feet in diameter. If you cannot find a tree thick enough, cut two or three lengths of a smaller one; lay the thickest log on the ground first, about ten or twelve feet in front of the tent; drive two strong stakes behind it, slanting a little backward; and lay the other logs on top of the first, resting against the stakes.

Now you are ready for the hand chunks, or andirons. These are shorter sticks of wood, eight or ten inches thick, laid at right angles to the backlog, four or five feet apart. Across these you are to build up the main firewood.

Use a dry spruce tree, not one that has fallen but one that is dead and still standing, if you want a lively, snapping fire. Use a hard maple or a hickory if you want a fire that will burn steadily and make few sparks. But if you like a fire to blaze up at first with a splendid flame and then burn on with an enduring heat far into the night, a young white birch with the bark on is the tree to choose. Six or eight round sticks of this laid across the hand chunks, with perhaps a few quarterings of a larger tree, will make a glorious fire.

Use the match first to touch off a roll of birch bark held in your hand. Then, when the bark is well alight, crinkling and curling, push it under the heap of kindlings, give the flame time to take a good hold, and lay your wood over it, a stick at a time, until the whole pile is blazing. Now your fire is started. Your friendly little red-haired gnome is ready to serve you through the night.

He will dry your clothes if you are wet. He will cheer you up if you are sad. He will spread an air of camaraderie through the camp and draw the men together in a half circle for story telling and jokes and singing. He will hold a candle for you while you spread your blankets on the boughs and dress for bed. He will keep you warm while you sleep—at least till about three o'clock in the morning, when you dream that you are out sleighing in your pajamas and wake up with a shiver.

The Cooking Fire

Of course, such a fire as I have been describing can be used for cooking, when it has burned down a little and there is a bed of hot embers in front of the backlog. But correct kitchen fires should be constructed in another way. What you want now is not a blaze but concentrated heat. You must be able to get close to your fire without burning your boots or scorching your face.

If you have the time and the material, make a fireplace of big stones. But not of granite, for that will split with the heat and perhaps fly in your face. If you are in a hurry and there are not suitable stones at hand, lay two good logs nearly parallel with each other, a foot or so apart, and build your fire between them. For a cooking fire, use split wood in short sticks. Let the first supply burn to glowing coals before you begin. A frying pan that is lukewarm one minute and red-hot the next can be very frustrating. If you want black toast, have it made before a fresh, sputtering heap of wood.

With fires, as with people, an excess of energy is a lack of usefulness. The best work is done without many sparks. Just enough is the right kind of a fire and a feast.

To know how to cook is a mundane skill. Yet there are times and seasons when it certainly seems to come in better than familiarity with the dead languages or much skill upon the lute, especially in the wilds.

You cannot always rely on your guides for a tasteful preparation of food. Many of them are ignorant of the differences between frying and broiling, and their notion of boiling a potato or a fish is to reduce it to a pulp. Now and then you find a man who has a natural inclination to the culinary art and who does very well within familiar limits.

Old Edouard, the Montaignais Indian who cooked for my friends last summer on the *Ste. Marguérite en bas,* was such a man. But Edouard could not read, and the only way he could tell the nature of canned provisions was by the pictures on the cans. If the picture was strange to him, there was no guessing what he would do with the contents of the can. He was capable of roasting strawberries and serving green peas cold for dessert. One day a can of mulligatawny soup and a can of apricots were handed to him simultaneously and without explanation. Edouard solved the problem by opening both cans and cooking them together. We had a new soup that day, *mulligatawny aux apricots.* It was not as bad as it sounds. It tasted somewhat like chutney.

The real reason why food that is cooked over an open fire tastes so good to us is because we are really hungry when we get it. The man who serves up provisions for camp has a great advantage over the dealers who must satisfy the pampered appetite of people in houses. I never can get any bacon in New York like that which I buy at a little shop in Quebec to take into the woods. If I ever set up in the grocery business, I shall try to get a good trade among anglers. It will be easy to please my customers.

The Smudge Fire

The smudge owes its existence to the pungent mosquito, the bloodthirsty blackfly, and the peppery midge. To what the smudge fire owes its English name I do not know; but its French name means simply a thick, nauseating, intolerable smoke.

The smudge is called into being for the very purpose of creating a smoke of this kind, which is as disagreeable to the mosquito, the blackfly, and the midge as it is to the man whom they are devouring. But the man survives the smoke, while the insects succumb to it, being destroyed or driven away. Therefore, the smudge, dark and bitter in itself, frequently becomes, like adversity, sweet in its uses. It must be regarded as a form of fire with which man has made friends under the pressure of a cruel necessity.

It would seem as if it ought to be the simplest affair in the world to light up a smudge. And so it is— if you are not trying.

An attempt to produce almost any other kind of a fire will bring forth smoke abundantly. But when you deliberately undertake to create a smudge, flames break from the wettest timber, and green moss blazes with a furious heat. You hastily gather handfuls of seemingly incombustible material and throw it on the fire, but the flames increase. Grass and green leaves hesitate for an instant and then flash up like tinder. The more you put on, the more your smudge rebels against its proper task of smudging. It makes a pleasant warmth, to encourage the blackflies; and bright light to attract and cheer the mosquitoes. Your effort is a brilliant failure.

The proper way to make a smudge is this. Begin with a very little, lowly fire. Let it be bright but not ambitious. Don't try to make it smoke yet.

Then gather a good supply of stuff that seems likely to suppress fire without smothering it. Moss of a certain kind will do, but not the soft, feathery moss that grows so deep among the spruce trees. Half-decayed wood is good; spongy, moist, unpleasant stuff, a vegetable wet blanket. The bark of dead evergreen trees is better still. Gather a plentiful store of it. But don't try to make a smoke yet.

Let your fire burn a while longer; cheer it up a little. Get some unquenchable coals aglow in the heart of it. Don't try to make a smoke yet.

Now pile on your smoldering fuel. Fan it with your hat. Kneel down and blow it, and in ten minutes you will have a smoke that will make you wish you had never been born.

That is the proper way to make a smudge. But the easiest way is to ask your guide to make it for you.

With my eyes shut, I can call up a vision of eight birch bark canoes floating side by side on Moosehead Lake on a fair June morning fifteen years ago. They are anchored off Green Island, riding easily on the long, gentle waves. In the stern of each canoe is a guide with a long-handled net; in the bow, an angler with a light fly rod; in the middle, a smudge-fire kettle, smoking steadily. In the air to the windward of the little fleet hovers a swarm of flies drifting down on the shore breeze, with bloody purpose in their breasts but baffled by the protecting smoke of the smudge fire. In the water to the leeward side plays a school of speckled trout, feeding on the minnows that hang around the sunken ledges of rock. As a larger wave than usual passes over the ledges, it lifts the fish up, and you can see the big fellows, three, four, even five pounds apiece, poising themselves in the clear brown water. A long cast will send the fly over one of them. Let it sink a foot. Draw it up with a fluttering motion. Now the fish sees it and turns to catch it. There is a yellow gleam in the depth, a sudden swirl on the surface; you strike sharply and the trout is matching his strength against the spring of your four ounces of split bamboo.

You can guess at this size as he breaks water by the breadth of his tail: a pound of weight to an inch of tail—that is the traditional measure, and it usually comes pretty close to the mark, at least in the case of large fish. But it is never safe to record the weight until the trout is in the canoe. As the Canadian hunters say, "Sell not the skin of the bear while he carries it."

Now the breeze that blows over Green Island drops away, and the smoke of the eight smudge kettles falls like a thick curtain. The canoes, the dark shores of Norcross Point, the twin peaks of Spencer Mountain, the dim blue summit of Katahdin, the dazzling sapphire sky, the flocks of fleece-white clouds shepherded on high by the western wind, all have vanished. With closed eyes I see another vision, still framed in smoke—a vision of yesterday.

It is a wild river flowing into the Gulf of St. Lawrence, far down toward Labrador. There is a long, narrow, swift pool between two parallel ridges of rock. Over the ridge on the right pours a gush of pale yellow foam. At the bottom of the pool, the water slides down into furious rapids and dashes straight through an impassable gorge half a mile to the sea. The pool is full of salmon, leaping merrily in their delight at coming into their native stream. The air is full of blackflies, rejoicing in the warmth of the July sun. On a slippery point of rock, below the fall, are two anglers, tempting the fish and enduring the flies. Behind them is an old hut with a mighty column of smoke rising.

Through the cloud pillar that keeps back the insect host, you see the waving of a long rod. A silver-gray fly with a barbed rail darts out across the pool, swings around with the current, well under water, and slowly works past the big rock in the center just at the head of the rapid. Almost past it, but not quite, for suddenly the fly disappears, the line begins to run out, the reel sings sharp and shrill, and a salmon is hooked.

But how well is he hooked? That is the question. This is no easy pool to play a fish in. There is no chance to jump into a canoe and drop below him, and get the current to help you in drowning him. You cannot follow him along the shore. You cannot even lead him into quiet water, where your assistant can creep near to him unseen and drag him in with a quick stroke. You must fight your fish to a finish, and all the advantages are on his side. The current is terribly strong. If he makes up his mind to go downstream to the sea, the only thing you can do is to hold him by main force; and then it is ten-to-one odds that the hook tears out or the leader breaks.

It is not in human nature for one man to watch another handling a fish in such a place without giving advice. "Keep the tip of your rod up. Don't let your reel overrun. Stir him up a little, he's sulking. Don't let him 'jig,' or you'll lose him. You're playing him too hard. There, he's going down the rapid!"

Of course, the man who is playing the salmon does not like this. If he is quick-tempered, sooner or later he tells his counselor to shut up. But if he is a gentle, Christian kind of a man, wise as a serpent and harmless as a dove, he follows the advice that is given to him, promptly and exactly. Then, when it is all ended and he has seen the big fish, with the line over his shoulder, poised for an instant on the crest of the first billow of the rapid, and has felt the leader stretch and give and *snap!*—then he can have the satisfaction, while he reels in his slack line, of saying to his friend, "Well, old man, I did everything just as you told me. But I think if I had pushed that fish a little harder at the beginning, *as I wanted to,* I might have saved him."

The smoke of the smudge fire is sharp and tearful, but a man can learn to endure a good deal of it when he can look through its rings at such scenes as these.

The Little Friendship Fire

There are times and seasons when the angler has no need of any outdoor fires. He sleeps in a house. His breakfast and dinner are cooked for him in a kitchen. He is in no great danger from blackflies or mosquitoes. All he needs now, as he sets out to spend a day on the Neversink or the Swiftwater is a good lunch in his pocket and a little friendship fire to burn pleasantly beside him while he eats his frugal fare and prolongs his noonday rest.

This form of fire does less work than any other in the world. Yet it is far from being useless; and I would be sorry to live without it. Its only use is to make a visible center of interest where there are two or three anglers eating their lunch together, or to supply a kind of companionship to a lone fisherman. It is kindled and burns for no other purpose than to give you the sense of being at home and at ease. Why the fire should do this I cannot tell, but it does.

You may build your friendship fire in almost any way that pleases you; but this is the way in which you shall build it best. You have no ax, of course, so you must look about for the driest sticks you can find. Do not seek them close beside the stream, for there they are likely to be water soaked; but go back into the woods a bit and gather a good armful of fuel. Then break it, if you can, into lengths of about two feet and construct your fire in the following fashion.

Lay two sticks parallel and put between them a pile of dried grass, dead leaves, small twigs, and the paper in which your lunch was wrapped. Then lay two other sticks crosswise on top of your first pair. Strike your match and touch your kindlings. As the fire catches, lay on other pairs of sticks, each pair crosswise to the pair that is below it, until you have a pyramid of flame. This is "a Micmac fire" such as the Indians make in the woods.

Now you can pull off your wading boots and warm your feet at the blaze. You can toast your bread if you like. You can even make an attempt to broil one of your trout, fastened on the end of a birch twig if you have a fancy that way. When your hunger is satisfied, you shake out the crumbs for the birds and squirrels, pick up a stick with a coal at the end to light your pipe, put some more wood on your fire, and settle down for an hour's reading if you have a book in your pocket or for a good talk if you have a comrade with you.

The stream of time flows swift and smooth by such a fire as this. The moments slip past unheeded; the sun sinks down the western arch; the shadows begin to fall across the brook; it is time to move on for the afternoon fishing. The fire has almost burned out. But do not trust it too much. Throw some sand over it or bring a hatful of water from the brook to pour on it, until you are sure that the last glowing ember is extinguished and nothing but the black coals and the charred ends of the sticks are left.

Even the little friendship fire must keep the law of the bush. All lights out when their purpose is fulfilled!

Altars of Remembrance

I like to go back to a familiar little river and fish or dream along the banks where I have dreamed and fished before. I know every bend and curve: the sharp turn where the water runs under the roots of the old hemlock tree; the snaky glen, where the alders stretch their arms far out across the stream; the meadow reach, where the trout are fat and silvery and will only rise about sunrise or sundown, unless the day is cloudy; the Naiad's Elbow, where the brook rounds itself, smooth and dimpled, to embrace a cluster of pink laurel bushes. All these I know; and almost every current and eddy and backwater I know long before I come to it. I remember where I caught the big trout the first year I came to the stream—and where I lost a bigger one. I remember the pool where there were plenty of good fish last year and wonder whether they are there now.

Better things than these I remember: the companions with whom I have followed the stream in days long past; the rendezvous with a comrade at the place where the rustic bridge crosses the brook; the hours of sweet conversation beside the friendship fire; the meeting at twilight with my fine lady and the children, who have come down by the wood road to walk home with me.

One May evening, a couple of years ago, I was angling in the Swiftwater and came upon Joseph Jefferson, stretched out on a large rock in midstream and casting the fly down a long pool. He had passed the threescore and ten years allotted to humans, but he was as eager and as happy as a boy in his fishing. "You here!" I cried. "What good fortune brought you into these waters?"

"Ah," he answered, "I fished this brook forty-five years ago. It was in the Paradise Valley that I first thought of Rip Van Winkle. I wanted to come back again for the sake of old times."

But what has all this do with an open fire? I will tell you. It is at the places along the stream, where the little flames of love and friendship have been kindled in bygone days, that the past returns most vividly. These are the altars of remembrance.

It is strange how long a small fire will leave its mark. The charred sticks, the black coals do not decay easily. If they lie well up the bank, out of reach of the spring floods, they will stay there for years. If you have chanced to build a rough fireplace of stones from the brook, it seems almost as if it would last forever.

There is a mossy knoll beneath a great butternut tree on the Swiftwater where such a fireplace was built four years ago; and whenever I come to that place now I lay the rod aside and sit down for a little while by the fast-flowing water and remember.

This is what I see: a man wading up the stream, with a basket over his shoulder, and perhaps a dozen trout in it; two little lads in gray corduroys running down the path through the woods to meet him, one carrying a frying pan and a kettle, the other a lunch sack on his arm. Then I see the bright flames leaping up in the fireplace and hear the trout sizzling in the pan and smell the appetizing odor. Now I see the lads coming back across the footbridge that spans the stream, with a bottle of milk from the nearest farm-house. They are laughing and teetering as they balance along the single plank. Now the table is spread on the moss. How good the lunch tastes! Never were there such pink-fleshed trout, such crisp and savory slices of broiled bacon. And after the lunch is finished and the bird's portion has been scattered on the moss, we creep carefully on our hands and knees to the edge of the brook and look over the bank at the big trout that is poising himself in the amber water. We have tried a dozen times to catch him but never succeeded. The next time, perhaps . . .

Well, the fireplace is still standing. The butternut tree spreads its broad branches above the stream. The violets and the bishop's-caps and the wild anemones are sprinkled over the banks. The yellowthroat and the water thrush and the vireos still sing the same tunes in the thicket. And the elder of my two boys often comes back with me to that pleasant place and shares my fisherman's luck beside the Swiftwater.

But the young boy?

Ah, my little Barney—my son who has passed into the next world—you have gone to follow a new stream, clear as crystal, flowing through fields of wonderful flowers that never fade. It is a strange river to Teddy and me; strange and very far away. Someday we shall see it with you; and you will teach us the names of those blossoms that do not wither. But till then, little Barney, the other lad and I will follow the old stream that flows by the woodland fireplace—your altar.

Rue grows here. Yes, there is plenty of rue. But there is also rosemary, that's for remembrance! And close beside it I see a little heart's ease. How fitting.

69

Christmass
Austriaca

CHRIS
IMHOF

CHAPTER 5

CHRISTMAS GREENS

(Written in Autumn)

The time draws near the birth of Christ"—a line from the poem *In Memoriam,* where the bells of four villages answer each other through the misty night while the wreaths of evergreen are woven with memories and regrets to deck the church and the home in honor of the best of all birthdays.

Once more the Yuletide is near—near at least to the one writing magazine articles, though by the dull, precise almanac it is still months away. For me it is proximate and pressing. The editor threatens; the printer waits at extra wages for overtime; tomorrow will be Christmas and the day after will be New Year's; and I must gather the symbolic greens today or leave our Christmas campfire without a token of remembrance or a sign of cheer.

But what a day is this on which I set about my pleasant task! Indian summer at its golden best: the blue sky subdued by a silvery haze to the tint of turquoise, faintly luminous; the fresh greenery of the woodlands, ripened and dulled a little by the August heat, now shot through with the first rich threads of autumnal glory; the mountains growing higher and more ethereal, as they recede in the light mist, until they change into bastions of amethyst; the deep blue of the open sea ever deepening far away, while the white flower of foam above the hidden reef expands and closes with every passing wave—a mystic lily on a sleeper's breast.

From every orchard the smell of ripening apples comes out to us, and from the tangled thicket we catch the odor of fox grapes, waiting for the frost to sweeten them. Wild asters and goldenrod adorn the wayside; gentians bloom in secret places. The little birds have assembled their silent companies for southward flight. But they are loath to leave their summer haunts, and, if we go warily through the wood, they will flock around us suddenly, fluttering through the thicket of trees in search of food, flitting from branch to branch on the dark firs, no doubt talking over their plans for the long journey to Central America.

All round us as we walk through this ephemeral beauty, the more enduring growths that are to serve for adornment in our homes at the midwinter festival are visible and suggestive to the inward eye that looks far ahead. Here the young spruces and balsam firs, shapely and symmetrical pyramids of absolute green, are standing by thousands in the open places—regiments of Christmas trees! Here the ground pines are made ready to be twined into garlands. Here the glistening, prickly holly lights its dark foliage with red berries; and the ground hemlock hides its delicate coral fruit like drops of translucent wax under its spreading branches; and the climbing bittersweet curls back its orange pods to show the scarlet-covered seeds within; and the pale-green mistletoe—a little farther south—prepares its pearly berries to sanction kisses yet unkissed.

Nature in her lavish way provides beauty for every season: flowers that fade and vanish as the summer goes; gold and crimson leaves that fall as the autumn wanes; and evergreens that will stay with us in rich and sober loveliness when full knee-deep lies the winter snow and the winter winds are wearily sighing. All these things are given us to enjoy. They are best in the place where nature put them, out-of-doors; but a little of each and all we may rightly take, if we will, to deck our dwellings, for no other purpose than to be a fragrant reminder that we humans are closer to nature than to our houses.

Shall we grieve, then, at the thought that some of these pretty, wild, growing things will be cut and gathered for Christmas greens? Not I—if the cutting and gathering are wisely done, with kindly forethought of the coming generations, so that no sort of harmless vine or amiable tree shall be exterminated from the earth.

To gather them prudently is to practice a kind of forestry. After all, one can think of no fairer way for a little fir tree to complete its life than by becoming for a while the sparkling center of a circle of human joy —a Christmas tree! If your imagination must endow the little fir with feelings, why not give it this fine emotion of ending in glory?

We are always looking backward and forward while we live the passing hour. Every true pleasure has in it an extract of the past and a tincture of the future. So it is with greens each Christmas.

One great artist said "all drawing of the things we see is an exercise of memory, and the things we have seen enter into it." The inspiration of poetry, Wordsworth found, has its origin in "emotion recollected in tranquillity." This is true both for sorrow and pure joy. There is not one little delight that comes to us without a flavor of reminder. When we lie on a bed of balsam boughs in the forest, we dream of a Christmas tree. When we enter the room where the gift-laden, lighted tree waits for the children, the very smell of it carries us away to camp in the greenwood. It works both ways.

There is no present reality for us humans, without memory and hope. Lose the first, and you are dead; lose the second, and you are buried. But in Christmas, as truly as in Easter, if we come to it in the proper spirit, there is a power of resurrection.

The custom of adorning our houses and places of worship at this season with green tokens from the winter woods came down to us, no doubt, from heathen ancestors who dwelt, as we do, in what is ironically called the north temperate zone. It was partly a tribute to unknown gods and partly an expression of man's wish to make himself comfortable and even merry in the teeth of the rudest weather.

In the tropics, of course, there would be no call for this defiance of the frost. And in the southern hemisphere the seasons would be reversed; instead of Christmas greens there would be a festival of flowers out-of-doors. There must be something charming in that; yet those who have tasted the ruder and more bracing joys of a northern Christmas always long for them and cannot be comforted with palms and pomegranates. Shakespeare, in *Love's Labour's Lost,* makes Biron say,

> At Christmas I no more desire a rose,
> Than wish a snow in May's new-fangled shows.

Some hold that the decking of houses with green branches in December originated among the Druids and was a pious provision for the poor wood spirits—elves and fays and good goblins—who needed a shelter from the nipping cold. That may be what the Druids told the people; but I think natural custom and a love of beauty had a good deal to do with it.

Holly with its bright sheen and vivid color was the symbol of mirth and good cheer. Ivy was sacred to Bacchus and hung over the door of wine shops; yet, if I mistake not, there was also an ancient tradition that whereas it invited to drinking it was also a talisman against drunkenness—a most considerate and helpful arrangement! Laurel and bay were signs of honor and festivity.

Mistletoe was the most weird and magical of all the Christmas greens, feared a little because of its association with druidical sacrifices, yet loved a good deal for its modern uses. They say that in the olden time it was allowed in the Yuletide decoration of houses but not churches. Yet in the eighteenth century, in York Cathedral, it was the custom on Christmas Eve to carry a branch of mistletoe to the high altar and "proclaim a public and universal liberty, pardon, and freedom to all sorts of inferior and even wicked people at the gates of the city toward the four quarters of heaven."

Nathaniel Hawthorne in his "English Note-Books" states,

> On Christmas Eve and yesterday, there were branches of mistletoe hanging in several parts of the house, in the kitchen, the entries, the parlor, and the smoking-room—suspended from the gas-fittings. The maids of the house did their utmost to entrap the gentlemen boarders, old and young, under the privileged places, and there to kiss them, after which they were expected to pay a shilling.

The old English customs and manners of Yule-tide—the general atmosphere of festive preparation, the caroling of the "waits" on Christmas Eve, the service in the village church on Christmas Morn, the feasting in servants' halls and dining room, the Yule log blazing on the broad hearth and the boar's head borne in with ceremony, the Wassail Bowl and the Christmas Pie, the songs and dances and games under the Lord of Misrule, the ghost stories by the fireside, the pervasive spirit of joviality and good comradeship between young and old, wise and simple, rich and poor—these Christmas charms are nowhere described more enchantingly than in *The Sketch-Book* of Washington Irving. No wonder that Sir Walter Scott loved the book and the author. Yet even when he wrote early in the nineteenth century Irving saw these customs as antiquities, in a vanishing light. He prefaced his essays with a quotation from a still earlier *Hue and Cry after Christmas*: "But is old, old, good old Christmas gone? Nothing but the hair of his good, gray, old head and beard left?"

In *Guesses at Truth,* written in 1827, I find this passage:

> It was a practice worthy of our ancestors to fill their houses at Christmas time with their relations and friends; that when Nature was frozen and dreary out of doors, something might be found within doors "to keep the pulses of their hearts in proper motion." The custom, however, is only appropriate among people who happen to have hearts.

I wonder what particular ways of our own day the people of the twenty-second century will regard as especially picturesque and romantic.

There is plenty about Christmas in the treasure house of English poetry, from Milton's glorious hymn to the lyrics of Eugene Field. Richest and most Christmas-like are the old ballads and carols and the poems by such writers as Robert Herrick. But every poet when he comes to this subject shows something of his own personal character and sentiment—his way of looking at life. Thus, Stevenson writes a ballad of *Christmas at Sea,* and Kipling of *Christmas in India.*

To some of us there is a peculiar brightness and sweetness in the memories associated with the hallowed household rites of putting up the greens and dressing the tree. This is done on Christmas Eve, after the younger children, or perhaps the grandchildren, have hung up their stockings and gone to bed. The elder children help. There is a joyous bustle and an air of secrecy about the business. If you hear a patter of small feet on the stair or see a tousled head peeping through the banisters, you must pretend to notice nothing.

The tall stepladder must be brought up from the cellar, and it is usually very rickety. There are wreaths to be hung in windows and garlands to be looped over doors. A new way of decorating the pillars is much called for, but after many experiments you always come back to the old way. Then the tree must be set up on a white cloth and decked with lights and hung with ornaments, old and new. Then the presents, the simpler the better, must be arranged in little piles under the tree.

Last of all, there are certain pictures—"the old familiar faces" gone away, but never nearer than tonight—and each one of them must have its wreath of green, or perhaps a flower in a little vase before it. While you are doing this you have few words but long thoughts.

Now it is midnight and so to bed, for the children will have emptied their stockings by sunrise and will be down in force to assault the room where the tree is locked in. This is Christmas at home—the best place.

Whatever turnings and overturnings, whatever calamity and ruin, are in store for this battered old world, you and I will never be poorer than the blessed Mary and Joseph when they walked to Bethlehem, and that same night

> The stars in the bright sky looked down where
> He lay—
> The little Lord Jesus asleep on the hay.

Whatever fantasies of government the brains of leaders may devise, the heart of humankind will always ask and take a day of rest and peace, gladness and goodwill to sweeten the long year.

So let us put up our bits of Christmas green, brothers and sisters, with brave and cheerful hearts; and if we want something to strengthen and steady us, we will read this verse of Charles Kingsley:

O blessed day, which giv'st the eternal lie
To self, and sense, and all the brute within;
O come to us amid this war of life;
To hall and hovel come: to all who toil,
In senate, shop, or study; and to those
Who sundered by the wastes of half a world,
Ill-warned and sorely tempted, ever face
Nature's brute powers, and men unmanned to brutes.
Come to them, blest and blessing, Christmas Day!
Tell them once more the tale of Bethlehem,
And kneeling shepherds, and the Babe Divine,
And keep them men indeed, fair Christmas Day.

CHAPTER 6

GOD OF THE OPEN AIR:
AN ODE

I

You who have made your dwelling fair
    With flowers below, above with starry lights
And set your altars everywhere—
    On mountain heights,
In woodlands dim with many a dream,
    In valleys bright with springs,
And on the curving capes of every stream:
You who have taken to yourself the wings
    Of morning, to abide
Upon the secret places of the sea,
    And on far islands, where the tide
Visits the beauty of untrodden shores,
Waiting for worshippers to come to be
    In thy great out-of-doors!
To you I turn, to you I make my prayer,
    God of the open air.

.　.　.　.　.　.　.　.　.

V

    But One, but One—ah, Son most dear,
And perfect image of the Love Unseen—
    Walked every day in pastures green,

And all his life the quiet waters by,
Reading their beauty with a tranquil eye.
To him the desert was a place prepared
    For weary hearts to rest;
    The hillside was a temple blest;
    The grassy vale a banquet room
Where he could feed and comfort many a guest.
    With him the lily shared
The vital joy that breathes itself in bloom;
And every bird that sang beside the nest
Told of the love that broods o'er every living thing.
    He watched the shepherd bring
His flock at sundown to the welcome fold,
    The fisherman at daybreak fling
His net across the waters gray and cold,
And all day long the patient reaper swing
His curving sickle through the harvest-gold.
So through the world the foot path way he trod,
Breathing the air of heaven in every breath;
And in the evening sacrifice of death
Beneath the open sky he gave his soul to God.
Him will I trust, and for my Master take;
Him will I follow; and for his dear sake,
    God of the open air,
    To you I make my prayer.

.   .   .   .

VII

.   .   .   .

    There are the things I prize
    And hold of dearest worth:
    Light of the sapphire skies,
    Peace of the silent hills,
Shelters of forest, comfort of the grass,
Music of birds, murmur of little rills,
Shadows of cloud that swiftly pass,

And, after showers,
The smell of flowers
And of the good brown earth—
And best of all, along the way, friendship and mirth.
So let me keep
These treasures of the humble heart
In true possession, owning them by love;
And when at last I can no longer move
Among them freely, but must part
From the green fields and from the waters clear,
Let me not creep
Into some darkened room and hide
From all that makes the world so bright and dear;
But throw the windows wide
To welcome in the light;
And while I clasp a well-beloved hand,
Let me once more have sight
Of the deep sky and the far-smiling land—
Then gently fall on sleep,
And breathe my body back to Nature's care,
My spirit out to you, God of the open air.

1904

PART 2

TRAVELS
HITHER AND YON

CHAPTER 7

A HANDFUL
OF HEATHER

My friend the avowed democrat expresses his scorn for monarchs (and his invincible love for his native Scotland) by renting, summer after summer, a famous castle among the heathery Highlands. There he proclaims the most uncompromising American point of view in a speech that grows more broadly Scotch with every week of his distance from the American accent of New York. He casts contempt on feudalism by playing the part of lord of the manor to such perfection and with such high-handed generosity that the people of the glen have become his clansmen. His gentle lady seems to be the patron saint of the district—if the Presbyterian theology of Scotland could only admit saints among the elect.

Every year he sends trophies of animals to his friends across the sea—birds that are as delicious and wild-flavored. He has a pleasant trick of making them pleasing to the imagination as well as to the palate by packing them in heather. I'll warrant that Aaron's rod bore no bonnier blossoms than these stiff little bushes—and none more magical. For every time I take up a handful of them they transport me to the Highlands and send me tramping once more, with knapsack and fishing rod, over the braes and down the burns.

Bell Heather

Most things taste best in the place where they were grown. And the scenery of a foreign land, including architecture, grows less dreamlike and unreal to our perception when we people it with familiar characters from our favorite novels. Even on a first journey we feel ourselves among old friends. To read *The Heart of Midlothian* in Edinburgh and *David Balfour* in the Pass of Glencoe and *The Pirate* in the Shetland Isles is to get a new sense of the possibilities of life. All these things I have done with much inward contentment; and similar things. But I never expect to pass pleasanter days than those I spent with *A Princess of Thule* among the Hebrides.

For then, to begin with, I was young. But even youth itself was not to be compared with the exquisite happiness of being deeply and desperately in love with Sheila, the clear-eyed heroine of that charming book.

King Arthur, the founder of the Round Table, expressed a conviction, according to Tennyson, that the most important element in a young knight's education is "the maiden passion for a maid." Surely the safest form in which this course may be taken is by falling in love with a girl in a book. It is the only affair of the kind into which a young man can enter without responsibility and out of which he can always emerge, when necessary, without discredit. And as for the old man who still keeps up this education of the heart and worships his heroine with great ardor, I maintain that he is exempt from all the penalties of declining years. The man who can love a girl in a book may be old but never aged.

So we sailed, lovers all three, among the Western Isles, and whatever ship it was that carried us, her figurehead was always the Princess Sheila. Along the ruffled blue waters of the sounds and lochs that wind among the roots of unpronounceable mountains and past the dark hills of the Isle of Skye and through the unnumbered flocks of craggy islets where the seabirds nest, the spell of the sweet Highland maid drew us, and we were pilgrims of the *Ulltima Thule* where she lived and reigned.

Lewis Island, with Harris Island as its tale, is quite sizable to be connected to such a country as Scotland. It is long and wide, and it has a large number of inhabitants compared to the other Hebride islands —and the conditions of agriculture and the fisheries are extremely interesting. All these I duly studied at the time and reported in a series of intolerably dull letters to the newspaper that supplied a financial basis for my sentimental journey. They are full of information, but I have been amused to note, after these many years, how widely they differ from the true motive and interest of that past trip. There is not even a hint of Sheila in any of them. Youth, after all, is a secretive season; it hides its real blossom underground.

It was Sheila's dark-blue dress and sailor hat with the white feather that we looked for as we wandered through the streets of Stornoway, that quaint metropolis of the herring trade, where strings of fish alternated with boxes of flowers in the windows and handfuls of fish were spread upon the roofs to dry just as the sliced apples are exposed upon the kitchen sheds of New England in September. Dark-haired women were carrying great creel of fish on their shoulders, and groups of sunburned men were smoking among the fishing boats on the beach and talking about fish. Sea gulls were floating over the houses with their heads turning from side to side and their bright eyes peering everywhere for unconsidered trifles of fish, and the whole atmosphere of the place—physical, mental, and moral—was pervaded with fish.

It was Sheila's soft, singsong Highland speech that we heard through the long, luminous twilight in the pauses of that friendly chat on the balcony of the little inn where a good fortune made us acquainted with Sam Bough, the mellow Edinburgh painter. It was Sheila's low sweet brow and long black eyelashes and tender blue eyes that we saw before us as we traipsed over the open moorland, a far-rolling sea of brown billows, reddened with patches of bell heather, and brightened here and there with little lakes lying wide open to the sky. Here were peatcutters, with the big baskets on their backs, walking in silhouette along the ridges, the people that Sheila loved and tried to help; and here were the crofters' cottages with thatched roofs, like beehives, blending almost imperceptibly with the landscape, the dwellings into which she planned to introduce the luxury of windows. Here were the Standing Stones of Callernish, huge tombstones of a vanished religion, the roofless temple from which the Druids paid their westernmost adoration to the setting sun as it sank into the Atlantic—and this was the place where Sheila picked the bunch of wild-flowers and gave it to her lover. There is nothing in history, I am sure, half so real to us as some of the events in fiction. The influence of an event upon our character is little affected by whether or not it ever happened.

There were three churches in Stornoway, all Presbyterian, of course, and therefore full of pious fervor. The idea of securing an American preacher for an August Sabbath seemed to fall upon them simultaneously. The brethren of the U.P. congregation arrived first at the inn and secured the promise of a morning sermon from Chancellor Howard Crosby. The session of the Free Kirk came a little later, and to them my father pledged himself for the evening sermon. The senior elder of the Established Kirk, a snuff-taking man and very deliberate, was the last to appear, and to his request for an afternoon sermon there was nothing left to offer but the services of the young novice in theology, namely, me. I could see that it struck him as a perilous adventure. Questions about "the fundamentals of the faith" glinted in his watery eye. He crossed and uncrossed his legs solemnly and blew his nose so frequently in a huge red silk handkerchief that it seemed like a signal of danger.

He secured an agreement with the father to accompany his son into the pulpit, so they appeared together in the church, a barnlike building with great galleries halfway between the floor and roof. Still higher up, the pulpit stuck out like a bird's nest against the wall. The two ministers climbed the precipitous stairs and found themselves in a box so narrow that one must be forced to stand while the other sat upon the only seat. In this uncomfortable fashion they went through the service. When it was time to preach, there was a quotation from the Song of Solomon, ending with "Sweet is thy voice, and thy countenance is comely." And when it came to that, the novice in theology's eyes (if the truth must be told) went searching through the sea of faces for one that should be familiar to his heart and to which he might make a personal application of the Scripture passage —even the face of Sheila.

There are rivers in the Lewis, at least two of them, and on one of these we had the offer of a rod for a day's fishing. We cast lots, and the lot fell upon the youngest. So I went forth with a tall, red-legged guide to try for my first salmon. The Whitewater came singing down out of the moorland into a rocky valley, and there was a delightful curl of air on the pools, and the silver fish were leaping from the stream.

The guide handled the big rod as if it had been a fairy's wand, but to me it was like a giant's spear. It was a very different affair from fishing with five ounces of split bamboo on a Long Island trout pond. The monstrous fly, like an awkward bird, went fluttering everywhere but in the right direction. It was the mercy of Providence that preserved the guide's life. But he was very patient and forbearing, leading me on from one pool to another, as I ruffled the water and snatched the hook out of the very mouth of rising fish, until at last we found a salmon that knew even less about the niceties of salmon fishing than I did.

He seized the fly firmly before I could pull it away, and then, in a moment, I found myself attached to a creature with the strength of a whale and the agility of a flying fish. He led me rushing up and down the bank like a madman. He played on the surface like a whirlwind and sulked at the bottom like a stone. He meditated, with tense delay, in the middle of the deepest pool and then, darting across the river, flung himself clean out of water and landed far up on the green turf of the opposite shore. My heart melted like a snowflake in the sea, and I thought that I had lost him forever. But he rolled quietly back into the water with the hook still set in his nose. A few minutes afterward I brought him within reach of the spear and my first salmon was glittering in the grass beside me.

Then I remembered that William Black had described this very fish in the *Princess of Thule*. I pulled the book from my pocket and sat down to read that delightful chapter over again. The breeze played softly down the valley. The warm sunlight was filled with the musical hum of insects and the murmur of falling waters. I thought how much pleasanter it would have been to learn salmon fishing as Black's hero did, from the Maid of Borva, than from a red-haired guide. But, then, his salmon, after leaping across the stream, got away, whereas mine was safe. A man cannot have everything in this world. I picked a spray of rosy bell heather from the bank of the river and pressed it between the leaves of the book in memory of Sheila.

Common Heather

I was on the way to a fishing tramp through Sutherlandshire. This northwest corner of Great Britain is the best place in the whole island for a modest and thrifty angler. There are, or there were a few years ago, wild lochs and streams that are still practically free, and a man who is content with small things can pick up some very scenic sport from the Highland inns and collect a rich basket of memorable experiences every week.

The inn at Lairg, overlooking the narrow waters of Loch Shin, was embowered in honeysuckles and full of creature comforts. But there were too many other men with rods there to suit my taste. "The fish in this lock," said the boatman, "is not so numerous as the fishermen, but more wise. There is not one of them that has not felt the hook, and they know ferry weel what side of the fly has the forked tail."

At Altnaharra, in the shadow of Ben Clebrig, there was a cozy little house with good fare and abundant trout fishing in Loch Naver. It was there that I fell in with a wandering pearl peddler who gathered his wares from the mussels in the moorland streams. These Scotch pearls had pretty, changeable colors of pink and blue upon them, like the iridescent light that plays over the heather in the long northern evenings. I thought it must be a hard life for the man, wading day after day in the ice-cold water and groping among the mossy, slippery stones for the shellfish and cracking open perhaps a thousand before he could find one pearl. "Oh, yes," said he, "and it is not an easy life, and I am not saying that it will be so warm and dry as living in a rich house. But it is the life that I am fit for, and I have my own time and my thoughts to myself, and that is a ferry good thing; and then, sir,

I haf found the Pearl of Great Price, and I think upon that day and night."

Upon the black, shattered peaks of Ben Laoghal, where I saw an eagle posing day after day as if some invisible centripetal force bound him forever to that small circle of air, there was a loch with plenty of brown trout and a few salmon; and down at Tongue there was a little river where the sea trout sometimes came up with the tide.

Here I found myself upon the north coast and took the road eastward between the mountains and the sea. It was a beautiful region of desolation. There were rocky glens cutting across the road, and occasionally a crawling stream ran down to the salt water, breaking the line of cliffs with a little bay and a half-moon of yellow sand. The heather covered all the hills. There were no trees and but few houses. The chief signs of human labor were the rounded piles of peat and the square cuttings in the moor, marking the places where the subterranean woodchoppers had gathered their harvest. Bricks of peat were then burned in the crofters' fireplaces.

The long valleys were once cultivated, and every patch of arable land had its group of cottages full of children. The human harvest has always been the richest and most abundant that is raised in the Highlands; but unfortunately the supply exceeded the demand; and so the crofters were evicted and great flocks of sheep were put in possession of the land. Now the sheep pastures have been changed into deer forests; and far and wide along the valleys and across the hills there is not a trace of habitation, except the heaps of stones and the clumps of straggling bushes that mark the sites of lost homes. But what is one country's loss is another country's gain. Canada and the United States are infinitely the richer because of the tough, strong, fearless, honest men that were dispersed from these lonely moors to make new homes across the sea.

White Heather

There is a nameless valley among the hills where you can still trace every curve of the stream and see the foam bells floating on the pool below the bridge and the long moss wavering in the current. There is a country song of a girl passing through the fields at sunset that still repeats its far-off cadence in your listening ears. There is a small flower trembling on its stem in some hidden nook beneath the open sky that never withers through all the changing year; the wind passes over it, but it is not gone—it abides forever in your soul, an unfading word of beauty and truth.

White heather is not an easy flower to find. You may look for it among the Highlands for a day without success. And when it is discovered, there is little outward charm to commend it. It lacks the grace of the dainty bells that hang so abundantly and the pink glow of the innumerable blossoms of the common heather. But it is a symbol. It is the Scotch *Edelweiss.* It means sincere affection and unselfish love and tender wishes as pure as prayers. I shall always remember the evening when I found the white heather on the moorland above Glen Ericht. Or, rather, it was not I that found it, but my companion, the gentle Mistress of the Glen, whose hair was whiter than the tiny blossoms and yet whose eyes were far quicker than mine to see and name every flower that bloomed in those lofty, widespread fields.

Ericht Water is formed by the marriage of two streams, one flowing out of Strath Ardle and the other descending from Cairn Gowar through the long, lonely Pass of Glenshee. The Ericht begins at the bridge of Cally, and its placid, beautiful glen, unmarred by railway or factory, reaches almost down to Blairgowrie. On the southern bank, but far above the water, runs the high road to Braemar and the Linn of Dee. On the other side of the river, nestling among the trees, is the low, white manor house, "An ancient home of peace." It is a place where one who had been wearied and perhaps deeply wounded in the battle of life might well desire to be carried, as Arthur to the island valley of Avalon, for rest and healing.

I have no thought of renewing the conflicts and cares that filled summer with sorrow. There was a touch of that wrath with those we love, which, as Coleridge says, "Doth work like madness in the brain"; and, flying from these troubles across the sea, I had found my old comrade of better days sentenced to death and caught but a brief glimpse of his pale, brave face as he went away into exile. At such a time the sun and the light and the moon and the stars are darkened, and the clouds return after rain. But through those clouds the Mistress of the Glen came to meet me—a stranger till then, but an appointed friend, a minister of needed grace, an angel of quiet comfort. The thick mists of rebellion, mistrust, and despair have long since rolled away, and against the background of the hills her figure stands out clearly, dressed in the fashion of fifty years ago, with the snowy hair gathered close beneath her widows's cap and a spray of white heather in her outstretched hand.

There were no other guests in the house by the river during those still days in the noontide hush of midsummer. Every morning, while the Mistress was busied with her household cares and letters, I would be out in the fields hearing the lark sing and watching the rabbits as they ran to and fro, scattering the dew from the grass in a glittering spray. Or perhaps I would be angling down the river with the swift pressure of the water around my knees and an inarticulate current of cooling thoughts flowing on and on through my brain like the murmur of the stream. Every afternoon there were long walks with the Mistress in the old-fashioned garden, where wonderful roses were blooming, or through the dark, fir-shaded den where the wild burn dropped down to join the river, or out upon the high moor under the waning orange sunset. Every night there were luminous and restful talks beside the open fire in the library, when the words came clear and calm from the heart, unperturbed by the vain desire of saying acceptable things.

One of the two should be a good listener, sympathetic, but not silent, giving confidence in order to attract it—and of this art a woman is the best master. But its finest secrets do not come to her until she has passed beyond the uncertain season of compliments and conquests and has entered into the serenity of a tranquil age.

What is this foolish thing that some say about the impossibility of true intimacy between the young and the old? Some would have us believe that a difference in years is a barrier between hearts. For my part, I have more often found it an open door of generous and tolerant welcome for the young soldier, who comes in tired and dusty from the battlefield, to tell his story of defeat or victory in the garden of still thoughts, where old age is resting in the peace of honorable discharge.

She spoke of the duty of being ready to welcome happiness as well as to endure pain and of the strength that endurance wins by being grateful for small daily joys, like the evening light and the smell of roses and the singing of birds. She spoke of the faith that rests on the Unseen Wisdom and Love like a child on its mother's breast and the melting away of doubts in the warmth of an effort to do some good in the world. And if that effort has conflict, adventure, mistakes, and even defeats mingled with it in the stormy years of youth, is not that to be expected? The burn roars and leaps in the den, and the stream chafes and frets through the rapids of the glen, and the river does not grow calm and smooth until it nears the sea.

Courage is a virtue that the young cannot spare; to lose it is to grow old before one's time. It is better to make a thousand mistakes and suffer a thousand reverses than to run away from the battle. Resignation is the courage of old age. It will grow in its own season, and it is a good day when it comes to us. Then there are no more disappointments; for we have learned that it is even better to desire the things that we have than to have the things that we desire. And is not the best of all our hopes—the hope of immortality—always before us? How can we be dull or heavy while we have that new experience to look forward to? It will be the most joyful of all travels and adventures. It will bring us our best acquaintances and friendships. But there is only one way to get ready for immortality, and that is to love this life and live it as bravely and cheerfully and faithfully as we can.

So my gentle teacher with the silver hair showed me the treasures of her ancient, simple faith; and I felt that no sermons, nor books, nor arguments can strengthen the doubting heart so deeply as just to come into touch with a soul that is founded upon a rock and has proved the truth of the simple faith whose highest philosophy is "Trust in the Lord and do good." At the end of the evening the household was gathered for prayers, and the Mistress kneeled among her servants, leading them in her soft Scottish accent through the old familiar petitions for pardon for the error of the day and refreshing sleep through the night and strength for the morrow.

I dare to hope that I have known something of the meaning of white heather since that evening when the Mistress of the Glen picked the spray and gave it to me on the lonely moor. "And now," she said, "you will be going home across the sea, and you have been welcome here, but it is time that you should go, for there is a place where your real duties and troubles and joys are waiting for you. And if you have left any misunderstandings behind you, you will try to clear them up; and if there have been any quarrels, you will heal them. Carry this little flower with you. It's not the bonniest blossom in Scotland, but it's the dearest, for the message that it brings. And you will remember that love is not getting, but giving; not a wild dream of pleasure, and a madness of desire—oh no, love is not that—it is goodness and honor and peace and pure living—yes, love is that. It is the best thing in the world, and the thing that lives longest. And that is what I am wishing for you and yours with this bit of white heather."

CHAPTER 8

AT THE SIGN
OF THE BALSAM BOUGH

> Come live with me, and be my love,
> And we will all the pleasures prove
> That valleys, groves, or hills, or field,
> Or Woods and steepy mountains yield.
>
> There we will rest our sleepy heads,
> And happy hearts, on balsam beds;
> And every day go forth to fish
> In foamy streams for ouananiche.
>
> *Old Song with a New Ending*

How can we go abroad without crossing the ocean, abandon an interesting family of children without getting completely beyond their reach, and escape from the frying pan of housekeeping without falling into the fire of the summer hotel? This apparently unsolvable problem we usually reconcile by camping in Canada.

It is indeed a foreign air that breathes around us as we make the harmless, friendly voyage from Point Levis to Quebec. The landlord of the quiet little inn on the outskirts of the town welcomes us with Gallic warmth as well-known guests and rubs his hands genially before us while he escorts us to our rooms, groping secretly in his memory to recall our names. We walk down the steep, quaint street to revel in the purchase of moccasins and waterproof coats and camping supplies.

But the true delight of the expedition begins when the tents have been set up in the forest back of Lake St. John and the green branches have been broken for the woodland bed and the fire has been lit under the open sky and, the fashionable street clothing being discarded, I sit down at a log table to eat supper with my special lady. Then life seems simple and amiable and well worth living. Then the uproar and confusion of the world die away from us, and we hear only the steady murmur of the river and the lovely voice of the wind in the treetops. Then time is long, and the only art that is needful for its enjoyment is short and easy. Then we taste true comfort while we lodge with Mother Nature at the Sign of the Balsam Bough under the stars.

Under the White Birches

Men may say what they will in praise of their houses and grow eloquent upon the merits of various styles of architecture, but, for our part, we are agreed that there is nothing to be compared with a tent. It is the most venerable and aristocratic form of human habitation. Abraham and Sarah lived in it and shared its hospitality with angels. It is exempt from the tyranny of the plumber, the painter, and the gas man. It is not immovably bound to one dull spot of earth by the chains of a cellar and a system of water pipes. It has a noble freedom of locomotion. It follows the wishes of its inhabitants and goes with them, a traveling home, as the spirit moves them to explore the wilderness. At their pleasure, new beds of wildflowers surround it, new plantations of trees overshadow it, and new avenues of shining water lead to its ever-open door. What the tent lacks in luxury it makes up for in liberty; liberty itself is the greatest luxury.

Another thing is worth remembering—a family that lives in a tent never can have a skeleton in the closet. They are so close, all secrets are revealed.

But not every spot in the woods is suitable for a camp, and good tenting-grounds must be chosen with knowledge and forethought. One of the necessities, indeed, is to be found everywhere in the St. John region. All the lakes and rivers are full of clear, cool water, and the traveler does not need to search for a spring. But it is always necessary to look carefully for a bit of smooth ground on the shore, far enough above the water to be dry, and slightly sloping, so that the head of the bed may be higher than the foot. Above all, it must be free from big stones and serpentine roots of trees. A root that looks no bigger than an inchworm in the daytime assumes the proportions of a boa constrictor at midnight—when you find it under your hipbone.

There should also be plenty of evergreens near at hand for the beds. Spruce has an aromatic smell; but it is too stiff and humpy. Hemlock is smoother and more flexible; but the spring soon wears out of it. The balsam fir, with its elastic branches and thick flat needles, is the best of all. A bed of these boughs a foot deep is softer than a mattress and as fragrant as a thousand Christmas trees. Two things more are needed for the ideal campground—an open environment where the breeze will drive away the flies and mosquitoes and an abundance of dry firewood within easy reach. Yes, and a third thing must not be forgotten, for, says the lady of my life, "I shouldn't feel at home in camp unless I could sit in the door of the tent and look out across flowing water."

All these conditions are met in our favorite camp-ing place below the first fall in the Grande Décharge. A rocky point juts out into the river and makes a fine landing for the canoes. There is a dismantled fishing cabin back in the woods, from which we can borrow boards for a table and chairs. A group of cedars on the lower edge of the point opens just wide enough to receive and shelter our tent. At a good distance be-yond ours, the guides' tent is pitched and the big campfire burns between the two dwellings. A pair of white birches lift their leafy crowns far above us, and after them we name the place *Le Camp aux Baouleaux.*

"Why not call trees people?—since, if you come to live among them year after year, you will learn to know many of them personally, and an attachment will grow up between you and them individually." So writes W. C. Prime, in his book *Among the Northern Hills,* and launches into praise on the white birch. And truly it is an admirable, lovable, and comfortable tree, beautiful to look upon and full of various uses. Its wood is strong to make paddles and ax handles and glorious to burn, blazing up at first with a flashing flame and then holding the fire in its glowing heart all through the night. Its bark is the most serviceable of all the products of the wilderness. In Russia, they say, it is used in tanning and gives its subtle, almost sacred fragrance to Russian leather. But here, in the woods, it serves more primitive ends. It can be peeled off in a huge roll from some giant tree and fashioned into a swift canoe to carry one over the waters. It can be cut into square sheets to roof his shanty in the forest. It is the paper on which he writes his woodland letters and the flexible material he bends into drinking cups of silver lined with gold. A basket for berries, a horn to call the lovelorn moose through the autumnal woods, a canvas on which to draw the outline of great and memorable fish—all these and many other indispensable luxuries are stored up for the skillful woodsman in the birch bark.

Only do not strip or mar the tree, unless you really need what it has to give you. Let it stand and grow in virgin majesty, uncurled and unscarred, while the trunk becomes a firm pillar of the forest temple and the branches spread all around a refuge of bright green leaves for the birds of the air. Nature never made a more excellent piece of handiwork. "And if," said my lady Greygown, "I should ever become a dryad, I would choose to be transformed into a white birch. And then, when the days of my life were numbered and the sap had ceased to flow and the last leaf had fallen and the dry bark hung around me in ragged curls and streamers, some wandering hunter would come in the wintry night and touch a lighted coal to my body, and my spirit would flash up in a fiery chariot into the sky."

The chief occupation of our idle days on the Grande Décharge was fishing. Above the camp spread a noble pool, more than two miles in circumference and diversified with smooth bays and whirling eddies, sand beaches and rocky islands. The river poured into it at the head, foaming and raging down a long chute, and swept out of it just in front of our camp in a merry, musical rapid. It was full of fish of various kinds—long-nosed pickerel, walleyed pike, and chub. But the prince of the pool was the fighting ouananiche, the little salmon of St. John. As Lancelot among the knights, so is the ouananiche among the fish, the plain-armored hero, the sunburnt champion of all the water folk.

Every morning and evening, Greygown and I would go out for ouananiche, and sometimes we caught plenty and sometimes few, but we never came back without a good catch of happiness.

At this season of the year, when summer is nearly ended, and every ouananiche in the Grand Décharge has tasted feathers and seen a hook, it is useless to attempt to delude them with the large gaudy flies the fishing tackle maker recommends. There are only two successful methods of angling now. The first of these I tried, and by casting delicately with a tiny brown trout fly tied on a gossamer strand of gut, I captured a pair of fish weighing about three pounds each. They fought against the spring of the four-ounce rod for nearly half an hour before Ferdinand could slip the net around them. With the second method, a grasshopper is attached to the hook, and, casting the line well out across the pool, Ferdinand put the rod into Greygown's hands. She stood posed upon a pinnacle of rock, like patience on a monument, waiting for a bite.

It came. There was a slow, gentle pull at the line, answered by a quick jerk of the rod, and a noble fish flashed into the air. Four pounds and a half at least! He leaped again and again, shaking the drops from his silvery sides. He rushed up the rapids as if he had determined to return to the lake, and down again as if he had changed his plans. He sulked in the deep water and rubbed his nose against the rocks. He did his best to treat that treacherous grasshopper as the whale served Jonah. But Greygown, through all her little screams and shouts of excitement, was steady and sage. She never gave the fish an inch of slack line; and at last he lay glittering on the rocks, with the black St. Andrew's crosses clearly marked on his plump sides and the iridescent spots gleaming on his small, shapely head.

"*Une belle!*" cried Ferdinand, as he held up the fish in triumph, "and it is madame who has the good fortune. She understands well to take the large fish—is it not?" Greygown stepped demurely down from her pinnacle, and as we drifted down the pool in the canoe under the mellow evening sky, her conversation betrayed not a trace of the pride that a victorious fisherman would have shown. On the contrary, she insisted that angling was an affair of chance—which was consoling, though I knew it was not altogether true—and that the smaller fish were just as pleasant to catch and better to eat, after all. For a generous rival, commend me to a woman. And if I must compete, let it be with one who has the grace to dissolve the bitterness of defeat in the honey of mutual self-congratulations.

We had a garden, and our favorite path through it was the portage leading around the falls. We traveled it very frequently, making an excuse of idle errands to the steamboat landing on the lake and sauntering along the trail as if school were out and would never begin again. It was the season of fruits rather than of flowers. Nature was reducing the decorations of her table to make room for the banquet. She offered us berries instead of blossoms.

There were the light coral clusters of the dwarf cornel set in whorls of pointed leaves; and the deep bluebells that the White Mountain people call the bearberry. There was the gray, crimson-veined berries for which the Canada Mayflower exchanged its feathery white bloom, and the ruby drops of the twisted stalk hanging like jewels along its bending stem. The partridge vine was full of rosy provision for the birds. The dark, tiny leaves of the creeping snowberry were all sprinkled over with delicate drops of spicy foam. There were a few late raspberries, and, if we chose to go out into the burnt ground, we could find blueberries in plenty.

But there was still bloom enough to give that festal air without which the most abundant feast seems coarse and vulgar. The pale gold of the loosestrife had faded, but the deeper yellow of the goldenrod had begun to take its place. The blue banners of the fleur-de-lis had vanished from beside the springs, but the purple of the asters was appearing. Closed gentians kept their secret hidden, and bluebells trembled above the rocks. The quaint pinkish-white flowers of the turtlehead showed in wet places, and instead of the purple-fringed orchids, which had disappeared with midsummer, we found now the slender braided spikes of the lady's tresses, latest and lowliest of the orchids, pale and pure as nuns of the forest and exhaling a celestial fragrance.

There is a secret pleasure in finding these delicate flowers in the rough heart of the wilderness. It is like discovering the veins of poetry in the character of a guide or a lumberman. And to be able to call the plants by name makes them a hundredfold more sweet and intimate. Naming things is one of the oldest and simplest of human pastimes. Children play at it with their dolls and toy animals. In fact, it was the first game ever played on earth, for the Creator who planted the Garden eastward in Eden knew well what would please the childish heart of man when He brought all the new-made creatures to Adam "to see what he would call them."

Our rustic bouquet graced the table under the white birches while we sat by the fire and watched our four men at the work of the camp—Joseph and Raoul chopping wood in the distance; Francois slicing juicy strips from the side of bacon; and Ferdinand, the chef, heating the frying pan in preparation for supper.

"Have you ever thought," said Greygown, in a contented tone of voice, "that this is the only period of our existence when we attain to the luxury of a French cook?"

"And one with the grand manner, too," I replied, "for he never fails to ask what it is that madame desires to eat today, as if the larder of a king were at his disposal, though he knows well enough that the only choice lies between broiled fish and fried fish, or bacon with eggs and a rice omelet. But I like the fiction of a lordly ordering of the meal. How much better it is than having to eat what is flung before you at a summer boarding house by a scornful waitress!"

"Another thing that pleases me," continued my lady, "is the unbreakableness of the dishes. There are no nicks in the edges of the best plates here; and, oh! it is a happy thing to have a home without bric-a-brac. There is nothing here that needs to be dusted."

"And no engagements for tomorrow," I replied. "Dishes that can't be broken, and plans that can—that's the ideal of housekeeping."

"And then," added my philosopher in skirts, "it is certainly refreshing to get away from all one's relations for a little while."

"But how do you figure that out?" I asked in mild surprise. "What are you going to do with me?"

"Oh," said she, with a fine air of independence, "I don't count you. You are not a relation, only a connection by marriage."

"Well, my dear," I answered, "it is good to consider the advantages of our present situation. We shall soon come into the frame of mind of the Sultan of Morocco when he camped in the Vale of Rabat. The place pleased him so well that he stayed until the very pegs of his tent took root and grew up into a grove of trees around his pavilion."

Kenogami

The guides were a little restless under the idle lifestyle of our lazy camp and urged us to set out upon some adventure. So Ferdinand led us on to seek the famous fishing grounds of Lake Kenogami.

We skirted the eastern end of Lake St. John in our two canoes and pushed up La Belle Rivèire to Hebertville, where all the children turned out to follow our procession through the village. It was like the train that tagged after the Pied Piper of Hamelin. We embarked again, surrounded by an admiring throng, at the bridge where the main street crossed a little stream and paddled up it through a score of backyards and a stretch of reedy meadows, where the wild and tame ducks fed together. We crossed the placid Lac Vert and, after a carry of a mile along the highroad toward Chicoutimi, turned down a steep hill and pitched our tents on a crescent of silver sand, with the long, fair water of Kenogami before us.

It is amazing to see how quickly these woodsmen can make a camp. Each one knew precisely his share of the enterprise. One sprang to chop a dry spruce log into fuel for a quick fire and fell a tree to keep us warm through the night. Another stripped a pile of boughs from a balsam for the beds. Another cut the tent poles from a neighboring thicket. Another unrolled the bundles and made the cooking utensils ready. As if by magic, the miracle of the camp was accomplished. "The bed was made, the room was fit,/ By punctual eve the stars were lit," said the poet Stevenson.

Our permanent camp was another day's voyage down the lake, on a beach opposite the Point Ausable. But the fish were shy and furtive. Old Castonnier, the guardian of the lake, lived in his hut on the shore and flogged the water, early and late, every day with his homemade flies. He was anchored in his dugout close beside us and grinned with delight as he saw his overeducated trout refuse my best casts. "They are there, M'sieu', for you can see them," he said, by way of discouragement, "but it is difficult to take them. Do you not find it so?"

In the back of my fly book I discovered a tiny phantom minnow—a dainty affair of varnished silk, as light as a feather—and quietly attached it to the leader in place of the tail fly. Then the fun began.

One after another the big fish dashed at that deception, and we played and netted them, until our score was thirteen, weighing altogether thirty-five pounds, and the largest five and a half pounds. The guardian was mystified and disgusted. He looked on for a while in silence and then pulled up anchor and clattered ashore. He must have made some inquiries and reflections during the day, for that night he paid a visit to our camp. After telling bear stories and fish stories for an hour or two by the fire, he rose to depart and, tapping his forefinger solemnly upon my shoulder, expressed himself as follows: "You can say a proud thing when you go home, M'sieu'—that you have beaten the old Castonnier. There are not many fishermen who can say that."

Our tent was on the border of a gathering of young trees. It was pleasant to be awakened by an assembly of birds at sunrise and to watch the shadows of the leaves dance out upon our translucent roof of canvas.

All the birds in the bush are early in the season, but there are so many of them that it is difficult to believe that every one can be rewarded with a worm. Here in Canada those little people of the air who appear as transient guests of spring and autumn in the Middle States are in their summer home and breeding place. Warblers, named for the magnolia and the myrtle, chestnut-sided, bay-breasted, blue-backed, and black-throated, flutter and creep along the branches with simple lisping music. Kinglets, ruby-crowned and golden-crowned, tiny, brilliant sparks of life, twitter along the trees, breaking occasionally into clearer, sweeter songs. Companies of redpolls and crossbills pass chirping through the thickets, busily seeking their food. The fearless, familiar chickadee repeats his name happily, while he leads his family to explore every nook and cranny of the wood. The beautiful tree sparrows and the pine siskins are more melodious, and the slate-colored juncos, flitting about the camp, are as talkative as chippy birds. All these varied notes come and go through the tangle of morning dreams. And now the noisy blue jay is calling "Thief—thief—thief!" in the distance, and a pair of great woodpeckers with crimson crests are laughing loudly in the swamp over some family joke. Then there is that harsh creaking note, the cry of the northern shrike, of whom tradition says that he catches little birds and impales them on sharp thorns. At the sound of his voice the concert closes suddenly and the singers vanish into thin air. The hour of music is over; the commonplace of day has begun. And there is my lady, Greygown, already up and dressed, standing by the breakfast table and laughing at my late appearance.

The Island Pool

Among the mountains there was a gorge, and in the gorge there was a river with a pool. In that pool there was an island where for four happy days there was a camp.

It was by no means an easy matter to settle ourselves in that lonely place. The river, though not re-

mote from civilization, is practically inaccessible for
nine miles of its course by reason of the steepness of
its banks, which are long, shaggy precipices, and the
fury of its current, in which no boat can survive. We
heard its voice as we approached through the forest
and could hardly tell whether it was far away or near.

There is a dimension to sound as well as to sight,
and one must have some idea of the size of a noise
before one can judge its distance. A mosquito's horn
in a dark room may seem like a trumpet on the battle-
ments; and the tumult of a mighty stream heard
through an unknown stretch of woods may appear
like the babble of a mountain brook close at hand.

But when we came out upon the bald forehead of
a stark cliff and looked down, we realized the gran-
deur and beauty of the unseen voice that we had been
following. A river of splendid strength went leaping
through the chasm five hundred feet below us, and at
the foot of two snow-white falls, in an oval of dark
topaz water, traced with curves of floating foam, lay
the solitary island.

The broken path was like a ladder. "How shall
we ever get down?" sighed Greygown, as we dropped
from rock to rock; at the bottom she looked up sighing, "I know we never can get back again." There was
not a foot of ground on the shores level enough for a
tent. Our canoe ferried us over, two at a time, to the
island.

The ouananiche fish in the island pool were superb, astonishing, incredible. We stood on the cobblestones at the upper end, and cast our little flies
across the sweeping stream, and for three days the fish
came crowding in to fill the barrel of pickled salmon

for our guides' winter use; and the score rose—twelve, twenty-one, thirty-two; and the size of the "biggest fish" steadily mounted—four pounds, four and a half, five, five and three-quarters. "Precisely almost six pounds," said Ferdinand, holding the scales; "but we may call him six, M'sieu', for if it had been tomorrow that we had caught him, he would certainly have gained the other ounce."

Why should I repeat the fisherman's folly of writing down the record of that marvelous catch? We always do it, but we know that it is a vain thing. Few listen to the tale, and none accept it. Does not Christopher North, reviewing the *Salmonia* of Sir Humphry Davy, openly mock and jeer at the fish stories of that most reputable writer? But on the very next page old Christopher himself meanders on into a perilous narrative of the day he caught a whole cartload of trout in a Highland loch. Incorrigible, happy inconsistency! Slow to believe others and full of skeptical inquiry, the man never doubts one belief that somewhere in the world a tribe of readers will be discovered to whom his fish stories will appear credible.

One of our days on the island was Sunday—a day of rest in a week of idleness. We had a few books; for there are some in existence that will stand the test of being brought into close contact with nature. Are not John Burroughs's cheerful essays full of woodland truth and companionship? Can you not carry a whole library of lyrical philosophy in your pocket with Matthew Arnold's volume of selections from Wordsworth?

But to be very frank about the matter, the camp is not stimulating to the studious side of my mind. Charles Lamb, as usual, has said what I feel: "I am not much a friend to out-of-door reading. I cannot settle my spirits to it."

There are blueberries growing abundantly among the rocks—huge clusters of them, bloomy and luscious as the grapes of Eshcol. The blueberry is nature's compensation for the ruin of forest fires. It grows best where the woods have been burned away and the soil is too poor to raise another crop of trees. Surely it is a carefree pleasure to wander along the hillsides gathering these wild fruits, as the Master and His disciples once walked through fields and plucked the ears of corn, never caring what the Pharisees thought of that new way of keeping the Sabbath.

There is a bed of moss beside a dashing rivulet, inviting us to rest and be thankful. There is also a white-throated sparrow on a little tree across the river, whistling his afternoon song. Down in Maine they call him the Peabody bird, because his notes sound to them like—*Péabody, péabody, péabody.* In New Brunswick the Scotch settlers say that he sings—*Kénnedy, kénnedy, kénnedy.* But here in his northern home I think we can understand him better. He is singing again and again—*Cánada, cánada, cánada!* The Canadians, when they came across the sea, remembering the nightingale of southern France, baptized this little gray minstrel their *rossignol,* and the country ballads are full of his praise. Every land has its nightingale, if we only have the heart to hear him. How distinct his voice is—how personal, how confidential, as if he had a message for us!

There is a breath of fragrance on the cool shady air beside our little stream that seems familiar. It is the first week of September. Can it be that the twin-flower of June, the delicate *Linnoea borealis*, is blooming again? Yes, here is the threadlike stem lifting its two frail pink bells above the bed of shining leaves. How dear an early flower seems when it comes back again and unfolds its beauty in an Indian summer! How delicate and suggestive is the faint, magical odor! It is like a renewal of the dreams of youth.

"And need we ever grow old?" asked my lady Greygown, as she sat that evening with the twin-flower on her breast, watching the stars come out along the edge of the cliffs and tremble on the hurrying tide of the river. "Must we grow old as well as grey? Is the time coming when all life will be commonplace and practical and governed by a dull 'of course'? Shall we not always find adventures and romances, and a few blossoms returning, even when the season grows late?"

"At least," I answered, "let us believe in the possibility, for to doubt it is to destroy it. If we can only come back to nature together every year and consider the flowers and the birds and confess our faults and mistakes and our unbelief under these silent stars and hear the river murmuring our absolution, we shall die young, even though we live long; we shall have a treasure of memories that will be like the twin-flower, always a double blossom on a single stem, and carry with us into the unseen world something that will make it worthwhile to be immortal."

CHAPTER 9

BETWEEN THE LUPIN
AND THE LAUREL

An English writer has written a delightful book of interviews with birds and other wild things, which bears the attractive title *Within an Hour of London Town*. But I would not publish the name of the hiding place so that the careless, fad-following crowd should not flock there and spoil it. Let the precious secret be communicated only by word of mouth or by letter, in a confidence and as a gift of friendship, so that none but the like-minded may hit the trail to the next-door remnant of Eden.

It was in this way that my four friends—Quakers in creed as well as in deed—told me as I was toiling over my numberless examination papers, their secret find of a little river in South Jersey, less than an hour from Philadelphia, where one could float in a canoe through mile after mile of unbroken woodland and camp at night in a bit of wilderness as wildly fair as when the wigwams of the Lenni-Lenape Indians were hidden among its pine groves. The Quakers said that they "had a concern" to guide me to their delectable retreat and that they hoped the "way would open" for me to come.

Canoes and tents and camp-kit? "That will all be provided: it is well not to be anxious concerning these minor things."

Mosquitoes? "Concerning this, also you must learn to put your trust in Providence; yet there is a happy time between the fading of the hepatica and the blooming of the mosquito, when the woods of South Jersey are habitable for man, and it would be most prudent to choose this season for the exercise of providential trust regarding mosquitoes."

Examination papers? Duty? "Surely thee must do what thee thinks will do most good, and follow the inward voice. And if it calls thee to stay with the examination papers or if it calls thee to go with us, whichever way, thee will be resigned to obey."

Fortunately, there was no doubt about the inward voice; it was echoing the robins; it was calling me to go out like Elijah and dwell under a juniper tree. I replied to the Quakers in the words of one of their own preachers: "I am resigned to go, or resigned to stay, but most resigned to go"; and we went.

Our good temper was imperturbable; for had we not all "escaped as a bird from the hand of the fowler" —Master Thomas from the mastery of his famous boarding school in Old Chester, and Friends Walter and Arthur from the uninspired scripture of their ledgers and day-books, and I from the incubation of those hideous examination papers, and the gentle Friend William from his—I have forgotten what particular monotony William was glad to get away from, but I know it was from something similar. I could read it in his face, in his pleased, communicative silence, in the air of almost reckless abandon with which he took off his straight-breasted Quaker coat and started out in his shirtsleeves to walk with Walter ahead of the cart that carried our two canoes and the rest of us over to the river.

It was just an ordinary express wagon, with two long, heavy planks fastened across the top of it. On these the canoes were lashed, with their prows projecting on either flank of the huge horse, who turned his head slowly from one side to the other as he stalked along the level road and looked back at his new rural environment with wonder. The driver sat on the dashboard between the canoes; and Master Thomas, Arthur, and I were perched on the ends of the planks with our feet dangling over the road.

The road was uncompromisingly straight. It lay across the slightly undulating sandy plain like a long yellow ruler; and on each side were the neatly marked squares and parallelograms of the little truck farms, all cultivated by Italians. Their new and unabashed frame houses were freshly painted in incredible tones of carrot yellow, pea green, and radish pink. The few shade trees and the many fruit trees, with whitewashed trunks, were lined up in unbending regularity. The women and children were working in rows of strawberries that covered acre after acre of white sand with stripes of deep green. Some groups of people by the wayside were chattering merrily together in their native language. It was a scene of foreign industry and cheerfulness, a bit of little Italy transplanted. Only the landscape was distinctly not Italian, but South Jersey to the core. Yet the people seemed at home and happy in it. Perhaps prosperity made up to them for the loss of picturesque scenery.

A mile or so beyond this, the road dipped gently into a shallow, sparsely wooded valley and we came to a well-built stone bridge that spanned, with a single narrow arch, the little river of our voyage. It was like a big brook, flowing with deep, brown current out of a thicket and on through a small cranberry bog below the bridge. Here we launched and loaded our canoes and went down with the stream through a bit of brushy woodland till we found a good place for lunch. For though it was long past noon and we were hungry, we wanted to get into the woods before we broke bread together.

Scanty woods they were, indeed; just a few scrub pines growing out of a bank of clean white sand. But we spread a rubber blanket in their thin shade and set forth our repast of biscuits and smoked beef and olives and fell to eating as heartily as if it had been banquet. The yellow warblers and the song sparrows were flitting about us; and two catbirds and a yellowthroat were singing from the thicket on the opposite shore. There were patches of snowy sandy-myrtle and yellow poverty-plant growing around our table; tiny, hardy, heathlike creatures, delicately wrought with bloom as if for a king's palace. In a still arm of the stream, a few yards above us, was a clump of the long, naked flowerscapes of the golden club, not half entered upon their silvery stage.

It was strange what pleasure these small gifts of blossom brought to us. We were in the mood Wordsworth describes in the lines written in his pocket copy of "The Castle of Indolence":

There did they dwell, from earthly labour free,
As happy spirits as were ever seen;
If but a bird, to keep them company,
Or butterfly sate down, they were, I ween,
As pleased as if the same had been a Maiden-queen.

But our "earthly labour" began again when we started down the stream; for now we had clearly entered the long strip of wilderness that curtains its winding course. On either hand the thickets came down so close to the water that there were no banks left; just woods and water blending and the dark topaz current swirling and gurgling through a clump of bushes or round the trunk of a tree, as if it did not care what path it took so long as it got through. Alders and pussy willows, viburnums, clethras, chokecherries, swamp maples, red birches, and all sorts of trees and shrubs that are water-loving, made an intricate labyrinth for the stream to thread; and through the tangle, catbriers, blackberries, fox grapes, and poison ivy were interlaced.

Worst of all was the poison ivy, which seemed there to deserve its other name of poison oak, for it was more like a tree than a vine, flinging its knotted branches from shore to shore and thrusting its venomous blossoms into our faces. Walter was especially susceptible to the influence of this poison, so we put him in the middle of our canoe, and I, being a veteran and immune, took the bow paddle. It was no easy task to guide the boat down the swift current, for it was bewilderingly crooked, twisting and turning upon itself. Many a time it ran us deep into the alders or through a snarl of thorn-set vines or crowed us under the trunk of an overhanging tree. We glimpsed the sun through the young leaves, now on our right hand, now on our left, now in front of us, and now over our shoulders. After several miles of this curlie-wurlie course, the incoming of Penny Pot Stream on the left broadened the flowing trail a little. Not far below that, the Hospitality Branch poured in its abundant waters on the right, and we were floating easily down a fair, open river.

There were banks now, and they were fringed with green borders of aquatic plants, rushes, and marsh marigolds, and round-leaved pond lilies, and pointed pickerel weed. The current was still rapid and strong, but it flowed smoothly through the straight reaches and around the wide curves. On either hand the trees grew taller and more stately. The mellow light of afternoon deepened behind them, and the rich cloud colors of approaching sunset tinged the mirror of the river with orange and rose. We floated into a strip of forest. The stream slackened and spread out, broadening into the head of a pond. On the left, there was a point of high land, almost like a low bluff, rising ten or twelve feet above the water and covered with a grove of oaks and white pines. Here we beached our canoes and made our first camp.

A slender pole was nailed horizontally between two trees, and from this the shelter tent was stretched with its sloping roof to the breeze and its front open toward the pond. There was no balsam or hemlock boughs for the beds, so we gathered armfuls of fallen leaves and pine needles, and spread our blankets on this rude mattress. Arthur and Walter cut wood for the fire. Master Thomas and William busied themselves with the supper. There was a famous dish of scrambled eggs and creamed potatoes and bacon, and

I know not what else. We ate till we could eat no more, and then we sat in the wide-open tent, with the campfire blazing in front of us, and talked of everything under the stars.

Bedtime comes at last, even when you are lodging at the Sign of the Beautiful Star. There were a few quiet words read from a peace-giving book, and a few minutes of silent thought in fellowship, and then each man pulled his blanket round him and slept as if there were no troubles in the world.

Certainly there were none waiting for us in the morning; for the day rose fresh and fair, and we had nothing to do but enjoy it. After fishing for an hour or two to supply our larder, we paddled down the pond, which presently widened into quite a lake, ending in a long, low dam with trees growing all across it. Here was the forgotten village of Watermouth, founded before the Revolution and once the seat of a flourishing iron industry. It was now stranded between two railways and basking on the warm sand hills in a painless and innocent state of decay.

The manor house stood in spacious grounds sloping gently down to the southern shore of the lake, well planted with a variety of shade trees and foreign evergreens, but overgrown with long grass and straggling weeds. Master Thomas and I landed and strolled through the neglected lawn toward the house in search of a possible opportunity to buy some fresh eggs. The long, pillared veranda had French windows opening to the floor. The wide double door opened into a central hall where a number of small signs told us that the mansion had already seen its best days of comfort and elegance. But there were other signs—a pillar leaning out of line, a bit of railing sagging down, a board loose at the corner. In a fragment of garden at one side, where a broken trellis led to an arbor more than half hidden by vines, we saw a lady, clad in black, walking slowly among the bewildered roses and clumps of hemerocallis, stooping now and then to pluck a flower or tenderly to lift and put aside a straggling branch.

We greeted her, stated our names and our occupations, and described the voyage that had brought us to Watermouth, in a way that led naturally to an explanation of our present need and desire for fresh eggs. The lady in black received us with gracious dignity, identified and placed us without difficulty (indeed she knew some relation of each of us), and gave us hospitable assurance that our wants in the matter of eggs could easily be satisfied. In the meantime she invited us to come up to the house with her and rest.

Rest was not an imperative necessity for us just then, but we were glad to see the interior of the old mansion. There was the long drawing room, with its family portraits running back into the eighteenth century, and the library, with its tall bookshelves was now empty. The lady in black was rather sad, for her father, a distinguished publicist and man of letters, had built this house; and her grandfather, a great iron-master, had owned most of the land nearby. The roots of her memory were all entwined about the place; but now she was dismantling it and closing it up, preparing to go away, perhaps to consider selling the estate.

By this time the tin pail had come in, filled with eggs. So we said farewell to the lady in black, recognizing her courtesy and kindness and with some silent reflections on the decline of family fortunes. Here had been a fine estate, a great family, a prosperous industry firmly established, now fading away like smoke. But I do not believe the lady in black will ever disappear entirely from Watermouth while she lives; for there is the old meeting house, a hundred years old (with the bees' nest in the weather boarding), for her to watch over, and care for, and worship in.

The young men were waiting for us below the dam. Here was splendid water-power running on almost idle. The great iron forge, with its massive stone buildings, stands (if the local tradition is correct) on the site where the first American cannonballs had been cast for the Revolutionary War.

It was here, on the slopes of the open fields and on the dry sides of the long embankment, that we saw the faded remnants of the beauty with which the lupins had surrounded Watermouth a few days ago. The innumerable plants with their delicate palm leaves were still fresh and vigorous; no drought can wither them even in the driest soil, for their roots reach down to the hidden waters. But their winged blossoms, which shortly before had "blued the earth," as Thoreau says, were now almost all gone; as if a countless flock of blue butterflies had taken flight and vanished. Only here and there one could see little groups of belated flowers, scraps of the indigo color, like patches of deep-blue sky seen through the rents in a drifting veil of clouds.

But the river called us away from the remembrance of the lupins to follow the promise of the laurels.

How charming was the curve of that brown, foam-flecked stream, as it rushed swiftly down, from pool to pool, under the ancient, overhanging elms and willows and sycamores! We gave ourselves to the current and darted swiftly past the row of weather-beaten houses on the left bank into the heart of the woods again.

Here the forest was dense, lofty, overarching. The tall silver maple, the black ash, the river birch, the swamp white oak, the sweet gum and the sour gum, a score of other trees closed around the course of the stream as it swept along with full, swirling waters. The air was full of a diffused, tranquil green light, subdued yet joyous, through which flakes and beams of golden sunshine flickered and sifted downward, as if they were falling into some strange, ethereal medium —something half liquid and half aerial, midway between the atmosphere and the sill depth of a fair sea.

The spirit of enchantment was in the place; brooding in the delicate, luminous midday twilight; hushing the song of the strong-flowing river to a humming murmur; casting a spell of beautiful immobility on the slender flower stalks and fern fronds and trailing shrubberies of the undergrowth. At the same time the young leaves of the treetops, far overhead, were quivering and dancing in the sunlight and the breeze. Here Shakespeare's fairy, Puck, might have a noontide council with Peaseblossom, Cobweb, Moth, and Mustardseed, speaking to them in whispers beneath the green and purple sounding board of a jack-in-the-pulpit flower.

There were many beautiful shrubs and bushes coming into bloom around us as we drifted down the stream. The Andromeda was now in its highest beauty, decorating the marshy grounds. The flowers are quite blood-red before they expand, but when full-grown the petals are flesh-colored. Andromeda is represented by them as a virgin of most exquisite and unrivaled charms. This plant is always fixed on some little turfy hillock in the midst of the swamps, as Andromeda herself was chained to the rock in the sea, which bathed her feet as the fresh water does the roots of the plant. Dragons and venomous serpents surrounded her, as toads and other reptiles frequent the abode of her vegetable namesake.

But more lovely than any of the shrubs along the river was that small tree known as the sweet bay or swamp laurel. It is not a laurel at all, but a magnolia, and its glistening leaves, dark green above, silvery beneath, are set around the large, solitary flowers at the ends of the branches, like backgrounds of metallic malachite, to bring out the perfection of a blossom carved in fresh ivory.

But it is not for us to penetrate into the secret of their love mystery. Leave that to the downy bee, the soft-winged moth, the flying beetle, who, seeking their own pleasure, carry the life-bestowing pollen from flower to flower. Our heavy hand would bruise the soft flesh and discolor its purity. Be content to feast your eyes upon its beauty and breathe its wonderful fragrance, floating on the air like the breath of love in the south and wild summer.

About the middle of the afternoon, after passing through miles of enchanted forest, unbroken by sign of human habitation, we came to a land in which it seemed always afternoon. Just beyond we made our second camp, on the point among the pines and the hollies. For here, at last, we were in the heart of the region of the laurels, which we had come to see. All along the river we had found some of them, just beginning to open their flowers, here and there.

I have seen the flame azaleas at their bright hour of full bloom in the hill country of central Georgia—lakes of tranquil and splendid fire spreading far away through the rough-barked colonnades of the pines. I have seen the thickets of great rhododendrons on the mountains of Pennsylvania in coronation week, when the magic of June covered their rich robes of darkest green with countless scepters, crowns, and globes of white bloom divinely tinged with rose: superb, opulent, imperial flowers. I have seen the Magnolia Gardens near Charleston, South Carolina, when their Arabian Nights' dream of color was unfolding beneath the dark cypresses and moss-bannered live oaks. I have seen the tulip and hyacinth beds of Holland rolled like a gorgeous carpet on the meadows beneath the feet of Spring; and the royal gardens of Kew in England in the month when the rose is queen of all flowers; but never have I seen an efflorescence more lovely, more satisfying to the eye, than that of the high laurel along the shores of the unknown little river of South Jersey.

Cool, pure, and virginal in their beauty, the innumerable clusters of pink and white blossoms thronged the avenues of the pine woods and ranged themselves along the hillsides and sloping banks and trooped down by cape and promontory to reflect their young loveliness in the flowing stream. It was as if some quiet and shadowy region of solitude had been suddenly invaded by companies of maidens attired for a holiday and joyously confident of their simple charms. The dim woodland was illumined with the blush of conscious pleasure.

Seen at a distance the flower clusters look like big hemispheres of flushed snow. But as I examined the laurels closely I noticed that each of the rounded blossoms was actually compounded of many separate blossoms—shallow, half-translucent cups poised on slender stems of pale green. The cup is white, tinted more or less deeply with rose-pink. The edge is scalloped into five points, and on the outer surface there are ten tiny projections around the middle of the cup within, each of these is a little red hollow made to receive a crimson tip, cunningly bent like a spring so that the least touch may loosen it and scatter pollen. There is no flower in the world more exquisitely fashioned than this. It is the emblem of a rustic maid in the sweet prime of her life.

We were well content with our day's voyage and our parting camp on the river. We had seen many lovely things and heard music from warbler and vireo, thrush and wren, all day long. Even now a wood thrush closed his last descant in flute-like notes across the river. Night began silently to weave her dusky veil upon the vast loom of the forest. The pink glow had gone from the flower-masses around us; whitely they glimmered through the deepening shadows and stood like gentle ghosts against the dark. Tomorrow we must paddle down to the village where the railroad crosses the river and hurry back to civilization and work. But tonight we were still very far off; and we will dream contentedly at the foot of a pine tree, beneath the stars, among the virgin laurels.

CHAPTER 10

TROUT FISHING
IN THE TRAUN

Ischl is about ten or twelve miles below Hallstatt, in the valley of the Traun. It is the fashionable summer resort of Austria. I found it in the high tide of amusement. The shady esplanade along the river was crowded with fashionable men and women; the hotels were overflowing; and there were various kinds of music and entertainments at all hours of the day and night. But all this did not seem to affect the fishing. The landlord of the Königin Elizabeth, who is also the mayor and a gentleman of varied accomplishments, kindly furnished me with a fishing license in the shape of a large pink card.

The easiest way, in theory, was to take the afternoon train up the river to one of the villages and fish down a mile or two in the evening, returning by the eight o'clock train. But in practice the habits of the fish interfered seriously with the latter part of this plan.

On my first day I had spent several hours in a vain effort to catch something better than small grayling. As the tail fly reached the middle of the water, a fine trout literally turned a somersault over it but without touching it. After casting for hours and taking nothing in the most beautiful pools, I landed three trout from one unlikely place in fifteen minutes. That was because the trout's supper time had arrived. So had mine. I walked over to the rambling old inn at Goisern, sought the cook in the kitchen, and persuaded her, in spite of the lateness of the hour, to boil the largest of the fish for my supper, then I rode peacefully back to Ischl by the eleven o'clock train.

The grayling has a quaint beauty. His appearance is aesthetic, like a fish in a pre-Raphaelite picture. His color in midsummer is a golden gray, darker on the back and with a few black spots just behind his gills, like patches put on to bring out the pallor of his complexion. He smells of wild thyme when he first comes out of the water. But the chief glory of the grayling is the large iridescent fin on his back. You see it cutting the water as he swims near the surface; and when you have him on the bank it arches over him like a rainbow. His mouth is under his chin, and he takes the fly gently, by suction.

Charles Cotton, the ingenious young friend of Izaak Walton of *The Compleat Angler* fame, was all wrong in calling the grayling "one of the deadest-hearted fishes of the world." He fights and leaps and whirls and brings his big fin to bear across the force of the current with a variety of tactics that would put his more aristocratic fellow-citizen, the trout, to blush. Twelve of these pretty fellows, with a brace of good trout for the top, filled my big creel to the brim. And yet, such is the inborn hypocrisy of the human heart that I always pretended to myself to be disappointed because there were not more trout and made light of the grayling as a thing of no account.

The pink fishing license did not seem to be of much use. Its presence was demanded only twice. Once a river guardian, who was walking down the stream with a Belgian Baron and encouraging him to continue fishing, climbed out to me on the end of a long embankment, and with proper apologies begged to be given a view of my document. It turned out that his request was a favor to me, for he discovered the fact that I had left my fly-book, with the pink card in it, beside the old mill, a quarter of a mile up the stream.

Another time I was sitting beside the road, trying to get out of a very long, wet, awkward pair of wading-stockings when a man came up to me in the dusk and accosted me with an absence of politeness that in German amounted to an insult.

"Have you been fishing?"

"Why do you want to know?"

"Have you any right to fish?"

"What right have you to ask?"

"I am a keeper of the river. Where is your card?"

"It is in my pocket. But, pardon my curiosity, where is your card?"

This question appeared to paralyze him. He had probably never been asked for his card before. He went lumbering off in the darkness, muttering, "My card? Unheard of! My card!"

The routine of angling at Ischl was varied by an excursion to the Lake of St. Wolfgang and the Schafberg, an isolated mountain on whose rocky horn an inn has been built. It stands up almost like a bird-house on a pole, and commands a superb view: north-

ward across the rolling plain and the Bavarian forest;
southward over rolling land of peaks and precipices.
There are many lovely lakes in sight, but the loveliest
of all is that which takes its name from the old saint
who wandered here from the country of the "furious
Franks" and built this peaceful hermitage on the Fal-
kenstine. What good taste some of those old saints had!

There is a venerable church in the village and a
chapel that is said to mark the spot where St. Wolfgang, who had lost his ax far up the mountain, found
it, like Longfellow's arrow, in an oak, and "still un-
broke." The tree is gone, so it was impossible to verify
the story. But the saint's well is there, in a pavilion,
with a bronze image over it and a useful inscription to
the effect that the poorer pilgrims "who have come
unprovided with either money or wine, should be jolly
well contented to find the water so fine." There is
also a famous echo farther up the lake, which repeats
six syllables with accuracy. It is a strange coincidence
that there are just six syllables in the name of "*der
heilige Wolfgang*." But when you translate it into English, the inspiration of the echo seems to be less ex-
act. The sweetest thing about St. Wolfgang was the
abundance of purple cyclamens, clothing the mountain meadows and filling the air with delicate fragrance like the smell of lilacs around a New England
farmhouse in early June.

There was still one stretch of the river above
Ischl left for the last evening's sport. I remember it so
well: the long, deep place where the water ran beside
an embankment of stone and the big grayling poised
on the edge of the shadow, rising and falling on the
current. There was the murmur of the stream and the

hissing of the pebbles underfoot in the rapids as the swift water rolled them over and over, the odor of the fir trees, and the streaks of warm air in quiet places, and the faint whiffs of wood smoke wafting from the houses, and the brown flies dancing heavily up and down in the twilight—surely it was all very good and a memory to be grateful for. And when the basket was full, it was pleasant to put off the heavy wading shoes and the long rubber stockings, and ride homeward in an open carriage through the fresh night air. That is as near to indulgent luxury as I should care to come.

The lights in the cottages are twinkling like fireflies, and there are small groups of people singing and laughing down the road. The honest fisherman reflects that this world is only a place of pilgrimage, but after all there is a good deal of cheer on the journey, if it is made with a contented heart. He wonders who the dwellers in the scattered houses may be and weaves romances out of the shadows on the curtained windows. The lamps burning in the wayside abodes tell him stories of human love and patience and hope, and of divine forgiveness. Dream-pictures of family life float before him tender and luminous, filled with a vague comfort.

Then the moon slips up into the sky from behind the eastern hills, and the fisherman begins to think of home and of the foolish, fond old rhymes about those whom the moon sees far away and the stars that have the power to fulfill wishes—as if the celestial bodies knew or cared anything about our small emotional reactions that we call affection and desires. But if there were Some One above the moon and stars who did know and care, Some One who could see the places

and the people that you and I would give so much to
see, Some One who could do for them all the kindness that you and I would hope to do, Some One able
to keep our beloved in perfect peace and watch over
the little children sleeping in their beds beyond the
sea—what then? Why, then, in the evening hour,
one might have thoughts of home that would go across
the ocean by way of heaven and be better than dreams,
almost as good as prayers.

CHAPTER 11

AMONG THE QUANTOCK HILLS

My little Dorothea was the only one of the carefree crowd who wished to turn aside with me from the beaten tourist track and give up the sight of another English cathedral for the sake of a quiet day among the Quantock Hills. Perhaps it was the literary association of that little corner of Somersetshire with the names of Wordsworth and Coleridge that attracted her. Or perhaps it was the promise that we would hire a dog cart, if one could be found, and that she should be the driver all through the summer day.

When she and I got off the railway carriage in the early morning at the humble station of Watchet (barely mentioned in the guidebook), our traveling companions jeered gently at our off-the-beaten-track excursion. As the train rumbled away from the platform, they stuck their heads out of the window and cried, "Where are you going? And how are you going to get there?" I did not know, and that was just the fun of it.

But there was an inn at Watchet, though I doubt whether it had ever entertained tourists. The friendly and surprised landlady thought that she could get us a dog cart to drive across the country; but it would take about an hour. So we strolled about the town and saw the sights of Watchet.

They were few and simple; yet something (perhaps the generous sunshine of the July day, or perhaps an inward glow of contentment in our hearts) made them bright and memorable. There were the quaint, narrow streets, with their tiny shops and low stone houses. There was the coast guard station, with its trim garden, perched on a terrace above the sea. There was the lifeboat house, with its doors wide open, and the great boat, spick-and-span in the glory of new paint, standing ready on its rollers and the record of splendid rescues in past years inscribed upon the walls. There was the circular basin harbor, with the workmen slowly repairing the breakwater and a couple of ancient-looking schooners reposing on their sides in the mud at low tide. And there, back on the hill, looking down over the town and far across the yellow waters of the Bristol Channel, was the high tower of St. Decuman's Church.

"It was from this tiny harbor," I said to Dorothea, "that a great friend of ours, the Ancient Mariner, set sail on a wonderful voyage. Do you remember?

> 'The ship was cheered, the harbor cleared,
>   Merrily did we drop
> Below the kirk, below the hill,
>   Below the lighthouse top.'

That was the church to which he looked back as he sailed away to an unknown country."

"But, Father," said Dorothea, "the Ancient Mariner was not a real person. He was only a character in Coleridge's poem!"

"Are you quite sure," said I, "that a character isn't a real person? Anyway, it was here that Coleridge, walking from Nether Stowey to Dulverton, saw the old sailor. And since Coleridge saw him, I reckon he lived, and still lives. Are we ever going to forget what he has told us?

> 'He prayeth best, who loveth best
>   All things both great and small;
> For the dear God who loveth us,
>   He made and loveth all.'"

Just then a most enchanting little boy and his sister, not more than five years old, came sauntering down the gray street, hand in hand. They were on their way to school, at least an hour late, round and rosy, the owners of the universe.

We could see them far down the street, pausing a moment to look in the shop windows or holding up their coppers while they stopped some casual passerby and made him listen to their story—just like the Ancient Mariner.

By this time the dog cart was ready. The landlord charged me eighteen shillings for the drive to Bridgewater, nineteen miles away, stopping where we liked, and sending back the cart with the post-boy that evening. So we climbed to the high seat, Dorothea took the reins and the whip, and we set forth for a day of pleasure not found in the guidebook.

What good roads they have in England! Look at the piles of broken stone for repairs, stored in little niches all along the way; see how promptly and carefully every hole is filled up and every break mended. A country with a fine system of roads is like a man with a good circulation of blood; the labor of life becomes easier, effort is reduced and pleasure increased.

Bowling along the smooth road, we crossed a small river at Doniford, where a man was wading the stream below the bridge and fly fishing for trout. We passed the farmhouses of Rydon, where the thresher was whirling and the wheat was falling in golden heaps and the pale-yellow straw was mounded in gigantic ricks; and then we climbed the hill behind St. Audries, with its pretty gray church and manor house half hidden in the great trees of the park.

The view was one of indescribable beauty and charm: soft, tranquil woods and placid, fertile fields; thatched cottages here and there, sheltered and embowered in green. Far away on the shore was the village of East Quantockshead, beyond that the broad, tossing waters of the Bristol Channel, and beyond that again, thirty miles away, the silver coast of Wales and the blue mountains fading into the sky. Ships were sailing in and out, toy-like in the distance. Far to the northwest, we could see the cliffs of the Devonshire coast; to the northeast the islands of Steep Holm and Flat Holm rose from the Severn Sea. Around the point beyond them, in the little churchyard of Clevedon, I knew that the dust of Arthur Henry Hallam, whose friendship with Tennyson was immortalized in "In Memoriam," was sleeping "By the pleasant shore/ And in the hearing of the wave."

High overhead the great white clouds were lingering across the deep-blue heaven. White butterflies wavered above the road. Tall foxglove spires lit the woodland shadows with rosy gleams. Bluebells and gold ragwort fringed the hedgerows. A family of young wrens fluttered in and out of the hawthorne. A yellowhammer, with cap of gold, warbled his sweet, common little song. The color of the earth was soft and red; the grass was of a green so living that it seemed to be full of conscious gladness. It was a day and a scene to calm and satisfy the heart.

At Kilve, a straggling village along the roadside, I remembered Wordsworth's poem called "An Anecdote for Fathers." The little boy in the poem says that he would rather be at Kilve than at Liswyn. When his father foolishly presses him to give a reason for his preference, he invents one: "At Kilve, there was no weather-cock,/ And that's the reason why." Naturally, I looked around the village to see whether it would still answer to the little boy's description. There was no weather-cock in sight, not even on the church tower, which is unusual.

Not far beyond Kilve we saw a white house, a mile or so away, standing among the trees to the south, at the foot of the high-rolling Quantock Hills. Our post-boy told us that it was Alfoxton, "where Must Wudswuth used to live," but just how to get to it he did not know. So we drove into the next village of Holford and made inquiry at the "Giles Plough Inn," a very quaint and rustic tavern with a huge ancient sign-board on the wall, representing Giles with his white horse and his brown horse and his plough. Turning right and left and right again, through narrow lanes, between cottages bright with flowers, we came to a wicket gate beside an old stone building,

145

and above the gate was a notice warning all persons not to trespass on the grounds of Alfoxton. But the gate was on the latch, and a cottager, passing by, told us that there was a "right of way" that could not be closed—"Goa straight on, and nivver fear, nubbody'll harm ye."

A few steps brought us into the thick woods and to the edge of a deep glen, spanned by a bridge made of a single long tree trunk, with a handrail at one side. Down below us, as we stood on the swaying bridge, a stream dashed and danced and sang through the shade, among the ferns and mosses and wildflowers. The steep sides of the glen glistened with hollies and laurels, tangled and confused with blackberry bushes. Overhead was the interwoven roof of oaks and ashes and beeches. Here it was that Wordsworth, in the year 1797, when he was working his way back from the despair that followed the shipwreck of his early revolutionary dreams, used to wander alone or with his dear sister Dorothy. And here he composed the "Lines Written in Early Spring"—almost the first notes of his new poetic power:

> I heard a thousand blended notes,
>   While in a grove I sat reclined,
> In that sweet mood when pleasant thoughts
>   Bring sad thoughts to the mind.
>
> Through primrose tuft, in that green bower,
>   The periwinkle trailed its leaves;
> And 'tis my faith that every flower
>   Enjoys the air it breathes.

Climbing up to the drive, we followed a long curving avenue toward the house. It led along the breast of the hill, with a fine view under the spreading arms of the great beeches, across the water to the Welsh mountains. On the left the woods were thick. Huge old hollies showed the ravages of age and storm. A riotous undergrowth of bushes and bracken filled the spaces between the taller trees. Doves were murmuring in the shade. Rabbits scampered across the road. In an open park at the edge of the wood, a herd of twenty or thirty fallow deer with pale spotted sides and twinkling tails trotted slowly up the slope.

Alfoxton House is a long, two-story building of white stone, with a pillared porch facing the hills. The back looks out over a walled garden, with velvet turf and brilliant flowers and pretty evergreens, toward the seashore. The house has been much changed and enlarged since the days when young William Wordsworth rented it (hardly more than a good farmhouse) for twenty-three pounds a year and lived in it with his sister from 1797 to 1798 in order to be near his friend Coleridge at Nether Stowey. There is not a room that remains the same, though the present owner has wisely brought together as much of the old woodwork as possible into one chamber, which is known as Wordsworth's study. But the poet's true place of work was out of doors; and it was there that we looked for the things that he loved.

In a field beyond the house there were two splendid old ash trees, which must have been full-grown in Wordsworth's day. We stretched ourselves among the gnarled roots, my little Dorothy and I, and fed our eyes upon the view that must have often refreshed him, while his Dorothy was leading his heart back with gentle touches toward the recovery of joy. There was the soft, dimpled landscape, in tones of silvery green, blue in distance, green near at hand, sloping down to the shining sea. The sky was delicate and friendly, bending close above us, with long lines of snowy clouds. There was hardly a breath of wind. Far to the east we saw the rich plain rolling away to Bridgewater and the bare line of the distant Mendip Hills. Shadows of clouds swept slowly across the land. Colors shifted and blended. On the steep hill behind us a row of trees stood out clear against the blue, with ships on the sea behind.

What induced Wordsworth to leave a place so beautiful? He was practically driven out by the suspicion and mistrust of his country neighbors. A poet was a creature with characteristics that they could not understand. His long rambles among the hills by day and night, regardless of the weather, his habit of talking to himself, his intimacy and his constant conferences on unknown subjects with Coleridge, whose radical ideas were no secret, were part of it. Also the rumor that the poet lived in France and sympathized with the Revolution—all these were dark and incriminating evidence to the unschooled mind that there was something wrong about this long-legged, sober-faced, careless young man. Probably he was a conspirator, plotting the overthrow of the English government. So went the talk of the countryside; and the lady who owned Alfoxton was so alarmed by it that she declined to harbor such a dangerous tenant any longer. Wordsworth went with his sister to Germany in 1798; and in the following year they found a new home at Dove Cottage in Grasmere, among the English lakes.

On our way out to the place where we had left our equipment, we met the owner of the estate, walking with his dogs. He walked with us to show the way up the "Harcknap"—the warpath of ancient armies— to a famous point of view. There we saw the Quantock Hills, rolling all around us. They were like long smooth steep billows of earth, covered with bracken and gorse and heather just coming into bloom. Thick woodlands hung on their sides, but above their purple shoulders the ridges were bare. They looked more than a thousand feet high. Among their cloven valleys, deep-thicketed and watered with cool springs, the wild red deer still find a home. And it was here that Wordsworth's old huntsman, "Simon Lee," followed the chase of the stage.

It was a three-mile drive from Holford to Nether Stowey. Dorothea remarked that Coleridge and the Wordsworths must have been great walkers if this was their idea of living close together. And so they were, for that bit of road seemed to them only a prelude to a real walk of twenty or thirty miles. The exercise put them in tune for poetry, and their best thoughts came to them when they were on foot.

"The George" at Nether Stowey is a very modest inn, the entrance paved with flagstones, the only public room a low-ceiled parlor; but its merits are far beyond its appearance. We lunched there most comfortably on roast duck and green peas, cherry tart and cheese, and then set out to explore the village, which is closely built along the roads whose junction is marked by a little clock tower. The market street is paved with cobblestones, and down one side of it runs a small brook, partly built in and covered over, but making a happy noise all the way. Coleridge speaks of it in his letters as "the dear gutter of Stowey."

Just outside town is the Castle Mound, a steep grassy hill, and we climbed to the top. There was the distinct outline of the foundations of the old castle, built in Norman times. We could trace the moat and the court and all the separate rooms; but not a stone of the walls remained—only a ground-plan drawn in the turf of the hilltop. All the pride and power of the Norman barons had passed like the clouds that were sailing over the smooth ridges of the Quantocks.

Coleridge was twenty-four years old when he came to Nether Stowey with his young wife and a baby boy. Troubles had begun to gather around him. He was very poor, tormented with neuralgia, unable to find a regular occupation, and estranged by a quarrel from his friend and brother-in-law, Robert Southey. Thomas Poole, a well-to-do tanner at Nether Stowey, a man of education and noble character, a great lover of poetry and liberty, had befriended Coleridge and won his deep regard and affection. Poole found a cottage near to his own house where the poet could live in quiet and friendly companionship.

The cottage was found, and, in spite of Poole's misgivings about its size, and his warnings in regard to the tedium and depression of village life, Coleridge took it and moved in with his little family on the last day of the year 1796. The young people came down Bridgewater Road through the wintry weather with their few household goods in a cart.

The cottage was at the western end of the village; and there it stands yet, a poor, ugly house, close by the street. We went in, and, after making clear to the good woman who owned it that we were not looking for lodgings, we saw all that there was to see of the dwelling. There were four rooms, two downstairs and two above. All were bare and disorderly, because, as the woman explained, housecleaning was in progress. She showed us a winding stair, hardly better than a ladder, which led from the lower to the upper rooms. There was no view, no garden. But in Coleridge's day there was a small plot of ground belonging to the house and running back to the large and pleasant place of his friend Poole.

It was upon this little garden that the imagination of the new tenant was fixed, and there he saw, in his dream, the corn and cabbages and the potatoes growing luxuriantly under his watchful and happy care. It would be enough, he hoped, to feed himself and his family and to supply a couple of what he called "snouted and grunting cousins."

"Literature," he wrote, "though I shall never abandon it, will always be a secondary object with me. My poetic vanity and my political favour have been exhaled, and I would rather be an expert, self-maintaining gardener than a Milton, if I could not unite them both." How unusual are men's dreams—those of humility as well as those of ambition!

In fact, I doubt whether the garden ever paid expenses; but, on the other hand, the crop of poetry that sprung from Coleridge's marvelous mind was rich and splendid. It was while he lived in this poor little cottage that he produced "Osorio," "Fears in Solitude," "Ode to France," the first part of "Christabel," "Frost at Midnight," "The Nightingale," "Kubla Khan," and "The Ancient Mariner," and planned

with his friend Wordsworth *Lyrical Ballads,* the most
epoch-making book of modern English poetry. Truly
this year, from April 1797 to April 1798, was the best
of his life. Never again was he so happy, never again
did he do such good work, as when he lived in his
cottage and slipped through the back gate to walk in
the garden or read in the library of his good friend
Thomas Poole or trudged down the road to the woods
of Alfoxton to talk with the Wordsworths. He wrote
lovingly of the place:

> And now, beloved Stowey, I behold
> Thy Church-tower, and methinks, the four huge elms
> Clustering, which mark the mansion of my friend;
> And close behind them, hidden from my view,
> Is my own lovely cottage, where my babe
> And my babe's mother dwell in peace.

Dorothea and I were not sure that Mrs. Coleridge enjoyed the cottage as much as he did. Greta
Hall, his house at Keswick, with its light airy rooms
and its splendid view, was her next home; and, when
we saw it a few weeks later, we were glad that the
babe and the babe's mother had lived there.

But the afternoon was waning, and we turned
our backs to the Quantocks and took to the road
again. Past the church and the manor house, with its
odd little turreted summerhouse, or gazebo, perched
on the corner of the garden wall, past a row of ancient larch trees and a grove of Scotch pines, past
smooth-rolling meadows full of cattle and sheep, past
green orchards full of fruit for the famous and potent
Somerset cider, past sleepy farms and spacious parks and
snug villas, we rolled along the high road into Bridge-

water, a small city where they make "Bath bricks" and where the statue of Admiral Blake swaggers sturdily in the marketplace. There we took the train to join our friends at dinner in Bristol; and so ended a most memorable day among the Quantock Hills.

PART 3

A JOURNEY WITHIN

CHAPTER 12

THE GARDEN, THE TEMPLE, AND THE TOMB

The Garden of Gethsemane

We traveled from the mount of Olives to the grove of olive trees, the Garden of Gethsemane, where Jesus used to take refuge with His friends. It lies on the eastern slope of Olivet, not far above the valley of Kidron, over against the city gate that was called the Beautiful, or the Golden, but which is now walled up.

The grove probably belonged to some friend of Jesus or to one of His disciples, who permitted them to make use of it for their quiet meetings. At that time, no doubt, the whole hillside was covered with olive trees, but most of these have now disappeared. The eight aged trees that still cling to life in Gethsemane have been enclosed with a low wall and an iron railing, and the little garden that blooms around them is cared for by Franciscan monks from Italy.

The gentle, friendly Fra Giovanni, in bare sandaled feet, coarse brown robe, and broad-brimmed straw hat, is walking among the flowers. He opens the gate for us and courteously invites us in, telling us in broken French that we may pick what flowers we like. I fell into a discussion with him in broken Italian, telling him of my visit years ago to the birthplace of his Order at Assisi. His old eyes soften into youthful brightness as he speaks of Italy. It was most beautiful, he said. *Bellisima!* But he is happier here, caring for this garden; it is most holy. *Santissima!*

The bronzed gardener, silent, patient, and absorbed in his task, moves with his watering pot among the beds, quietly refreshing the thirsty blossoms. There are wall flowers, stocks, pansies, baby's breath, pinks, anemones of all colors, rosemary, rue, poppies—all sorts of sweet old-fashioned flowers. Among them stand the scattered venerable trees, with enormous trunks, wrinkled and contorted, eaten away by age, patched and built up with stones, protected and tended with pious care, as if they were very old people whose life must be tenderly nursed and sheltered. Their trunks hardly seem to be of wood; so dark, so twisted and furrowed are they, and so enduring that they appear to be cast in bronze or carved out of black granite. Above each of them spreads a crown of fresh foliage, delicate, abundant, shimmering softly in the sunlight and the breeze. In the center of the garden is a kind of open flower house with a fountain of flowing water, erected in memory of a young American girl. At each corner a pair of slender cypresses lift their black-green spires against the blanched azure of the sky.

It is a place of refuge, of ineffable tranquillity, of unforgetful tenderness. The enclosure does not restrict us. How else could this sacred shrine of the out-of-doors be preserved? And what more fitting guardian for it than the Order of that loving Saint Francis, who called the sun and the moon his brother and his sister and preached to a joyous congregation of birds as his "little brothers of the air"? The flowers are lovely. Their ancient fragrance and gracious order mingle with the sorrows and sufferings of the place, transforming them into something beautiful. She grows her sweetest flowers in the ground that tears have made holy.

It is here, in this quaint and carefully tended garden, this precious place that has been saved alike from the oblivious trampling of the crowd and from the needless imprisonment of four walls and a roof, it is here in the open air, in the calm glow of the afternoon, under the shadow of Mount Zion, that we find for the first time that which we have come so far to seek—the soul of the Holy Land, the inward sense of the real presence of Jesus.

Nothing that we have yet seen in Palestine, no vision of a broad landscape, no sight of ancient ruin or famous building or treasured relic, comes as close to our hearts as this little garden sleeping in the sun. Nothing that we have read from our Bibles in the new light of this journey has been for us so suddenly illumined, so deeply and tenderly brought home to us, as the story of Gethsemane.

Here, indeed, in the moonlit shadow of these olives—if not of these very branches, yet of others sprung from the same immemorial stems—the deepest suffering was endured for humanity, the most profound sorrow of the greatest soul that loved all human souls. It was not in the temptation in the wilderness, as Milton imagined, that the crisis of the Divine life was enacted and Paradise was regained. It was in the agony in the garden.

Here the love of His own life wrestled in the heart of Jesus with the need of sacrifice, and the anguish of that wrestling wrung the drops of blood from Him like sweat. Here, for the only time, He found the cup of sorrow and shame too bitter and asked the Father to take it from His lips if it were possible—possible without breaking commitment, without surrendering love. For that He would not do, though His soul was exceeding sorrowful, even unto death. Here He learned the frailty of human friendship, the narrowness and dullness and coldness of the very hearts for whom He had done and suffered most, who could not even watch with Him one hour.

What infinite sense of the poverty and feebleness of humanity, the extent of selfishness, the uncertainty of the noblest of human aspirations and promises; what poignant questioning of the necessity, of self-destruction must have tortured the soul of Jesus in that hour! It was His black hour. None can imagine the depth of that darkness but those who have themselves passed through some of its outer shadows, in the times when love seems vain and sacrifice futile and friendship meaningless and life a failure and death intolerable.

Jesus met the spirit of despair in the Garden of Gethsemane; and after that meeting, the cross had no terror for Him because He had already endured them, the grave no fear because He had already conquered it. How calm and gentle was the voice with which He wakened His disciples, how firm the step with which He went to meet Judas! The bitterness of death was behind Him in the shadow of the olive trees. The peace of heaven shone above Him in the silent stars.

The Dome of the Rock

The oldest of the shrines of Jerusalem is the threshing floor of Araunah the Jebusite, which David bought from him as the future site of the Temple of Jehovah. No doubt the king knew of the traditions that connected the place with ancient and well-known rites of worship. But I think he was moved also by the commanding beauty of the area, on the very summit of Mount Moriah, looking down into the deep Kidron Valley.

Our way to this venerable and sacred hill leads through the crooked duskiness of David Street and across the half-filled depression of the Tyropoeon Valley that divides the city and up through the dim, deserted Bazaar of the Cotton Merchants, and so through the central western gate of the Haram-esh-Sherif, "the Noble Sanctuary."

This is a wide enclosure, clean, spacious, a place of refuge from the foul confusion of the city streets. The wall that shuts us in is almost a mile long, and within this open space, which has an immediate effect of expanse and tranquil order, are some of the most sacred buildings of Islam and some of the most significant landmarks of Christianity.

Slender and graceful arcades are outlined against the clear, blue sky: little domes are poised over praying places and ceremonial fountains; wide and easy flights of steps lead from one level to another in this sacred city.

At the southern end, beyond the tall cypresses and the splashing fountain fed from Solomon's Pools, stands the long Mosque el-Aksa. To Mohammedans, this is the place to which Allah brought their prophet from Mecca in one night; to Christians, it is the Basilica, which the Emperor Justinian erected in honor of the Virgin Mary. At the northern end rises the ancient wall of the Castle of Antonia, from whose steps Saint Paul, protected by the Roman captain, spoke his defense to the Jerusalem mob. The steps, hewn partly in the solid rock, are still visible; but the site of the castle is occupied by the Turkish barracks, beside which the tallest minaret of the Haram lifts its covered gallery high above the corner of the great wall.

Yonder to the east is the Golden Gate, above the steep valley of Jehoshaphat. Its entrance is closed with great stones because the Moslem tradition says that some Friday a Christian conqueror will enter Jerusalem by that gate. Not far away we see the column in the wall from which the Mohammedans believe a slender rope, or perhaps a naked sword, will be stretched, in the judgment day, to the Mount of Olives opposite. This, according to them, will be the bridge over which all human souls must walk, while Christ sits at one end, Mohammed at the other, watching and judging. The righteous, upheld by angels, will pass safely, whereas the wicked, heavy with unbalanced sins, will fall.

Dominating all these widespread relics and shrines, in the center of the enclosure, on a raised platform approached through delicate arcades, stands the great Dome of the Rock, built by Abd-el-Melik in 688 A.D., on the site of the Jewish Temple. The exterior of the vast octagon, with its lower half encased in marble and its upper half encrusted with Persian tiles of blue and green, its broad, round lantern and swelling black dome topped by a glittering crescent, is bathed in full sunlight—serene, proud, evoking a certain splendid simplicity. Within, the light filters dimly through windows of stained glass and falls on marble columns, bronzed beams, mosaic walls, screens of wrought iron and carved wood. We walk as if through an interlaced forest and undergrowth of rich entangled colors. It all seems visionary, unreal, fantastic, until we climb the bench by the end of the inner screen and look upon the Rock over which the Dome is built.

This is the original rock, a plain gray limestone, level and fairly smooth, the unchanged summit of Mount Moriah. Here the priest-king Melchizedek offered sacrifice. Here Abraham, in obedient faith, was about to slay his only Isaac because he thought it would please Jehovah. Here Araunah the Jebusite threshed his corn on the smooth rock and winnowed it in the winds of the hilltop, until King David stepped over from Mount Zion and bought the threshing floor and the oxen from him for fifty shekels of silver and built in this place an altar to the Lord. Here Solomon erected his splendid Temple and the Chaldeans burned it. Here Zerubbabel built the second Temple after the return of the Jews from exile and Antiochus Epiphanes desecrated it and Herod burned part of it and pulled down the rest. Here Herod built the third Temple, larger and more magnificent than the first, and the soldiers of the Emperor Titus burned it. Here the Emperor Hadrian built a

163

temple to Jupiter and himself, and someone, perhaps the Christians, burned it. Here Mohammed came to pray, declaring that one prayer was worth a thousand elsewhere. Here the Caliph Omar built a little wooden mosque and the Caliph Abd-el-Melik replaced it with this great one of marble and the Crusaders changed it into a Christian temple and Saladin changed it back again into a mosque.

This Haram-esh-Sherif is the second holiest place in the Moslem world. The Mohammedan pilgrims come here by the thousands, for the sake of their prophet. The Christian pilgrims come by thousands, for the sake of Him who said, "Neither in this mountain nor in Jerusalem shall you worship the Father." The Jewish pilgrims never come for fear their feet may unwittingly tread upon "the Holy of Holies" and defile it; but they creep outside the great enclosure, in the dark trench beside the foundation stones of the wall, mourning and lamenting for the majesty that is departed and the Temple that was once ground to powder.

But amid all these transitions and alterations stands the good old limestone rock, the threshing floor of Araunah, the capstone of the hill, waiting for the sun to shine and the dew to fall on it once more, as they did when the foundations of the earth were laid.

The legend says that you can hear the waters of the flood roaring in an abyss underneath the rock. I laid my ear against the rugged stone and listened. Was it the voice of turbulent centuries and the lapsing tide of men?

Golgotha

"We ought to go again to the Church of the Holy Sepulchre," said my beloved in a voice of dutiful reminder. "We have not seen half of it." So we went down to the heart of Jerusalem and entered the labyrinthine shrine.

The assorted crowd in the paved quadrangle in front of the double-arched doorway were buying and selling, bickering and chattering as usual. Within the portal, on a slightly raised platform to the left, the Turkish guardians of the holy places and keepers of the peace between Christians were seated among their rugs and cushions, impassive, idle, and dignified, drinking their coffee or smoking their tobacco, conversing gravely or counting their amber prayer beads. The Sultan owns the Holy Sepulchre; but he is a liberal host and permits all factions of Christendom to visit it and celebrate their rites in turn, provided only they do not disturb one another in their devotions. We saw his silent sentinels of tolerance scattered in every part of the vast, wandering structure.

The interior was dim and shadowy. Opposite the entrance was the Stone of Unction, a marble slab on which it is said the body of Christ was anointed when it was taken down from the cross. Pilgrim after pilgrim came kneeling to this stone, bending to kiss it beneath the Latin, Greek, Armenian, and Coptic lamps that hang about it by silver chains.

The Chapel of the Crucifixion was on our right, above us, in the second story of the church. We climbed the steep flight of stairs and stood in a little room, mysterious, crowded with lamps and icons and candelabra, encrusted with ornaments of gold and sil-ver, full of strange odors and glimmerings of mystic light. There, they told us, in front of that rich altar was the silver star that marked the place in the rock where the Holy Cross stood. And on either side of it were the pits that received the crosses of the two thieves. And a few feet away, covered by a brass slide, was the cleft in the rock made by the earthquake. It was lined with slabs of reddish marble and looked nearly a foot deep.

Priests in black robes and tall, cylindrical hats, and others with brown robes, rope belts and tonsured heads, were coming and going around us. Pilgrims were climbing and descending the stairs, kneeling and murmuring devotions, kissing the star and the cleft in the rock and the icons. Underneath us, though we were supposed to stand on the hill called Golgotha, were the offices of the Greek clergy and the Chapel of Adam.

We went around from chapel to chapel: into the opulent Greek cathedral where they show the "Cen-ter of the World"; into the bare little Chapel of the Syrians where they show the tombs of Nicodemus and Joseph of Arimathea; into the Chapel of the Appari-tion where the Franciscans say that Christ appeared to His mother after the Resurrection. There was sweet singing in this chapel and a fragrant smell of incense. We went into the Chapel of Saint Helena, under-ground, which belongs to the Greeks; into the Cha-pel of the Parting of the Raiment which belongs to the Armenians. We were impartial in our visit, but we did not have time to see the Abyssinian Chapel, the Coptic Chapel of Saint Michael, nor the Church of Abraham where the Anglicans are allowed to celebrate the eucharist twice a month.

The center of all this maze of creeds, ceremonies, and devotions is the Chapel of the Holy Sepulchre, a little church of precious marbles, carved and gilded, standing beneath the great dome of the church in the middle of a rotunda surrounded by marble pillars. We bought and lighted our wax candles and waited for a lull in the stream of pilgrims to enter the shrine. First, we stood in the vestibule with its tall candelabra, then in the Angels' Chapel, with its fifteen swinging lamps, making darkness visible; then, stooping through a low doorway, we came into the tiny chamber, six feet square, which is said to contain the rock-hewn tomb in which the Savior of the World was buried.

Rituals are celebrated here daily by different Christian sects. Pilgrims, rich and poor, come here from all parts of the habitable globe. They kneel beneath the forty-three hanging lamps of gold and silver. They kiss the worn slab of marble that covers the tombstone, some of them smiling with joy, some of them weeping bitterly, some of them with quiet, businesslike devotion as if they were performing a duty. The priest of their faith blesses them, sprinkles the relics that they lay on the altar with holy water, and one by one the pilgrims retire backward through the low portal.

I saw a Russian peasant, sad-eyed, wrinkled, bent with many sorrows, lay his cheek silently on the tombstone with a look on his face as if he were a child leaning against his mother's breast. I saw a little barefoot boy of Jerusalem with big, serious eyes, come quickly in and try to kiss the stone; but it was too high for him, so he kissed his hand and laid it upon the altar. I saw a young nun, hardly more than a girl, slender, pale, dark-eyed, with a noble Italian face, shaken with sobs, the tears running down her cheeks, as she bent to touch her lips to the resting place of the friend of sinners.

These are examples of the craving for penance, reverence, devotion, and some utterance of the nameless thirst and passion of the soul leads these pilgrims. It is at this place in which the divine mystery of sacrificial sorrow and death speaks to their hearts and comforts them.

Could any Christian of whatever creed, who could feel the trouble and longing of humanity, turn his or her back upon that altar? And yet in my deepest heart I was thirsty for the open air, the blue sky, the pure sunlight, the tranquillity of large and silent spaces.

My beloved went with me across the crowded quadrangle into the cool, clean, quiet German Church of the Redeemer. We climbed to the top of the lofty bell tower.

Jerusalem lay at our feet, with its network of streets and lanes, archways and convent walls, domes small and great—the black Dome of the Rock in the center of its wide enclosure, the red dome and the green dome of the Jewish synagogues on Mount Zion, the seven gilded domes of the Russian Church of Saint Mary Magdalen, a hundred tiny domes of dwelling houses, and right in front of us the yellow dome of the Greek "Center of the World" and the black dome of the Holy Sepulchre.

The quadrangle was still full of people buying and selling, but the murmur of their voices was faint and far away, less loud than the twittering of the thousands of swallows that soared and circled, with glistening of innumerable blue-black wings and soft sheen of white breasts, in the tender light of sunset above the facade of the gray old church.

Westward the long ridge of Olivet was bathed in the rays of the declining sun. Northward, beyond the city gate, the light fell softly on a little rocky hill, shaped like a skull, the ancient place of stoning for those the cruel city had despised and rejected and cast out. At the foot of that slope there is a quiet garden and a tomb hewn in the rock. Rosemary and rue grow there, roses and lilies; birds sing among the trees. Is not that little rounded hill, still touched with the free light of heaven, still commanding a clear outlook over the city to the Mount of Olives—is not that the true Golgotha, where Christ was lifted up?

As we were thinking of this we saw a man come out on the roof of the Greek "Center of the World" and climb by ladder up the side of the huge dome. He went slowly and carefully, yet with confidence, as if the task were familiar. He carried a lantern in one hand. He was going to the top of the dome to light up the great cross for the night. We spoke no word, but each knew the thought that was in the other's heart.

Wherever the crucifixion took place, it was surely in the open air, beneath the wide sky, and the cross that stood on Golgotha has become the light at the center of the world's night.

CHAPTER 13

THE SOURCE

(a Parable)

In the middle of the land that is called by its inhabitants Koorma and by strangers the Land of the Half-forgotten, I was toiling all day long through heavy sand and grass as hard as wire. Suddenly toward evening, I came upon a place where a gate opened in the wall of mountains, and the plain ran in through the gate, making a little bay of level country among the hills.

Now this bay was not brown and hard and dry, like the mountains above me; neither was it covered with tawny billows of sand like the desert along the edge of which I had wearily coasted. But the surface of it was smooth and green; and as the winds of twilight breathed across it they were followed by soft waves of greenery, with silvery turnings of the undersides of many leaves, like ripples on a quiet harbor. There were fields of corn, filled with silken rustling and vineyards with long rows of trimmed maple trees, each standing like an emerald goblet wreathed with vines, and flower gardens as bright as if the earth had been embroidered with threads of blue and scarlet and gold, and olive orchards frosted over with delicate and fragrant blossoms. Red-roofed cottages were scattered everywhere through the sea of greenery, and in the center, like a white ship surrounded by a flock of little boats, rested a small, fair, shining city.

I wondered greatly how this beauty had come into being on the border of the desert. Passing through the fields and gardens and orchards, I found that they were all encircled and lined with channels full of running water. I followed up one of the smaller channels until it came to a larger stream, and as I walked on beside it, still going upward, it guided me into the midst of the city, where I saw a sweet, beautiful river flowing through the main street, with an abundance of water and a very pleasant sound.

There were houses and shops and lofty palaces and all that makes a city, but the life and joy of all, and the one thing that I remember best, was the river. For in the open square at the edge of the city there were marble pools where the children might bathe and play. At the corners of the streets and on the sides of the houses, there were fountains for the drawing of water, and at every crossing a stream was turned aside to run out to the vineyards, and the river was the mother of them all.

There were but few people in the streets, and none of the older folk from whom I might ask counsel or a lodging; so I stood and knocked at the door of a house. It was opened by an old man, who greeted me with kindness and asked me to enter as his guest. After much courteous entertainment and when supper was ended, his friendly manner and attractiveness led me to tell him of my strange journeyings in the land

of Koorma and in other lands where I had been seeking the Blue Flower, the symbol of longing, and to
inquire of him the name and the story of his city and
the cause of the river that made it glad.

"My son," he answered, "this is the city that was
called Ablis, that is to say Forsaken. For long ago men
lived here, and the river made their fields fertile, and
their dwellings were full of plenty and peace. But because of many evil things that have been half-forgotten,
the river was turned aside, or else it was dried up at its
source in the high place among the mountains, so
that the water flowed down no more. The channels
and the trenches and the marble pools and the basins
beside the houses remained, but they were empty. So
the gardens withered and the fields were barren. The
city was desolate, and in the broken cisterns there
was little water.

"Then there came one from a distant country
who was very sorrowful to see the devastation. He
told the people that it was vain to dig new wells and
to keep the channels and trenches clean; for the water had come only from above. The Source must be
found again and reopened. The river would not flow
unless they traced it back to the spring and visited it
continually and offered prayers and praises beside it
without ceasing. Then the spring would rise to an
outpouring gush, and the water would run down plen-
tifully to make the gardens blossom and the city rejoice.

"So he went to open the fountain; but there were
few that went with him, for he was a poor man of
lowly account, and the path upward was steep and
rough. But his companions saw that as he climbed
among the rocks little streams of water gushed from

the places where he trod, and pools began to gather in the dry riverbed. He went more swiftly than they could follow him, and finally he traveled out of their sight. A little farther on they came to the rising of the river, and there, beside the overflowing Source, they found their leader lying dead."

"That was a strange story," I cried, "and it was very sad. Tell me how it happened, and what was the meaning of it."

"I cannot tell the whole of the meaning," replied the old man, after a little pause, "for it was many years ago. But this poor man had many enemies in the city, chiefly among the makers of water systems, who hated him for his words. I believe that they went out after him secretly and murdered him. But his followers came back to the city; and as they came the river began to run down very gently after them. They returned to the Source day by day, bringing others with them; for they said that their leader was really alive, though the form of his life had changed, and that he met them in that high place while they remembered him and prayed and sang songs of praise. More and more the people learned to go with them, and the path grew plainer and easier to find. The more the Source was revisited, the more abundant it became, and the more it filled the river. All the channels and the basins were supplied with water, and men made new channels that were also filled.

"Some of those who were diggers of trenches and diggers of wells said that it was their work that had brought about the change. But the wisest and best among the people knew that it all came from the Source, and they taught that if it should ever again be forgotten and left unvisited the river would fail again and drought return. So every day, from the gardens and orchards and the streets of the city, men and women and children have gone up the mountain path with singing, to rejoice beside the spring from which the river flows and to remember the one who opened it. We call it the River Carita. And the name of the city is no more Ablis, but Saloma, which is Peace. And the name of him who died to find the Source for us is so dear that we speak it only when we pray.

"But there are many things yet to learn about our city, and some that seem dark and cast a shadow on my thoughts. Therefore, my son, I bid you to be my guest, for there is a room in my house for any stranger; and tomorrow and on the following days you shall see how life goes with us and read, if you can, the secret of the city."

That night I slept well, as one who has heard a pleasant tale, with the murmur of running water woven through my dreams; and the next day I went out early into the streets, for I was curious to take part in the experience of visiting the Source.

Already the people were coming out and heading upward along the mountain path beside the river. Some of them went alone, swiftly and in silence. Others were in groups of two or three, talking as they went. Others were in larger companies, and they sang together with much joy and sweetness. But there were many people who remained working in their fields or in their houses or stayed talking on the corners of the streets. Therefore, I joined one of the men who walked alone and asked him why all the people did not go to the spring, since the life of the city depended on it, and whether, perhaps, the way was so long and so hard that none but the strongest could undertake it.

"Sir," he said, "I perceive that you are a stranger, for the way is both short and easy so that the children are those who most delight in it; and if a man were in great haste he could go there and return in a short time. But of those who remain behind, some are the busy ones who must visit the fountain at another hour. Some are the careless ones who take life as it comes and never think where it comes from, and others are those who do not believe in the Source and will hear nothing about it."

"How can that be?" I said. "Do they not drink of the water, and does it not make their fields green?"

"It is true," he said. "But these men have made wells close by the river, and they say that these wells fill themselves; and they have dug channels through their gardens, and they say that these channels would always have water in them even though the spring should cease to flow. Some of them say also that it is an unworthy thing to drink from a source that another has opened and that every man ought to find a new spring for himself. In this case they spend the hour of the vigil (and many more) in searching among the mountains where there is no path."

While I wondered about this, we kept walking along the way. There was already quite a throng of people all going in the same direction. And when we came to the Source, which flowed from an opening in a cliff, almost like a chamber cut in the rock, and made a little garden of wildflowers around it as it fell, I heard the music of many voices and the beautiful name of him who had given his life to find the forgotten spring.

Then we came down again, singing and in groups, following the river. It already seemed more bright and full and joyous. As we passed through the gardens I saw men turning aside to make new channels through the fields that were not yet cultivated. And as we entered the city I saw the wheels of the mills that ground the corn whirling more swiftly and the young women coming with their pitchers to draw from the brimming basins at the street corners and the children laughing because the marble pools were so full that they could swim in them. There was plenty of water everywhere.

For many weeks I stayed in the city of Saloma, going up the mountain path in the morning and returning to the day of work and the evening of play. I found friends among the people of the city, not only among those who walked together in the vigil of the Source, but also among those who remained behind, for many of them were kind and generous, faithful in their work, and very pleasant in their conversation.

Yet there was something lacking between me and them. I could not establish firm ground with them, for all their warmth of welcome and their pleasant ways. They were by their nature people who always dwell in one place; even their thoughts did not stray far. But I have always been a seeker, and the world seems to be made to wander in, rather than to stay in one corner of it and never see what the rest has in store. Now this was what the people of Saloma could not understand, and for this reason I seemed to them always a stranger, an alien, a guest. The fixed circle of their life was like an invisible wall, and with the best will in the world they did not know how to draw me within it. And I, for my part, while I understood well their wish to rest and be at peace, could not quite understand the way in which the desire found fulfillment, nor share the peace that seemed to them to be compete and lasting. In their gardens I always saw the same flowers, and none was perfect. At their feasts I always tasted the same food, and none of it made an end to hunger. In their talk I always heard the same words, and none that accompanied deep thought. The very tranquillity and single-mindedness perplexed and distanced me. What to them was permanent, to me was transient. They were inhabitants; I was a visitor.

The one in all the city of Saloma with whom I was most at home was Ruamie, the little granddaughter of the old man with whom I lodged. To her, a girl of fourteen, fair-eyed and full of joy, the novelty of life had not yet grown to routine. She was quick to feel and respond to the newness of every day that dawned. When a strange bird flew down from the mountains into the gardens, it was she who saw it and wondered at it. It was she who walked with me most often in the path to the Source. She went out with me to the fields in the morning and almost every day found wildflowers that were new to me. At sunset she drew me to happy games of children, where her fancy was never tired of inventing new additions to the familiar pastimes. In the dusk she would sit beside me in an arbor of honeysuckle and question me about the flower that I was seeking—for to her I had often spoken of my quest.

"Is it blue," she asked, "as blue as the speedwell that grows beside the brook?"

"Yes, it is as much bluer than the speedwell herb as the river is deeper than the brook."

"And is it bright," she asked, "as bright as the drops of dew that shine in the moonlight?"

"Yes, it is as much brighter than the drops of dew as the sun is clearer than the moon."

"And is it sweet," she asked, "as sweet as the honeysuckle when the day is warm and still?"

"Yes, it is as much sweeter than the honeysuckle as the night is stiller and more sweet than the day."

"Tell me again," she asked, "when you saw it, and why do you seek it?"

"Once I saw it when I was a boy, no older than you. Our house looked out toward the hills, far away and at sunset softly blue against the eastern sky. It was the day that we laid my father to rest in the little burying ground among the cedar trees. There was his father's grave and his father's father's grave, and there were the places for my mother and for my two brothers and for my sister and for me. I counted them all, when the others had gone back to the house. I paced up and down alone, measuring the ground. There was room enough for us all, and in the western corner where a young elm tree was growing—that would be my place, for I was the youngest. How tall would the elm tree be then? I had never thought of it before. It seemed to make me sad and restless—wishing for something, I knew not what—longing to see the world and to taste happiness before I must sleep beneath the elm tree.

"Then I looked off to the blue hills, shadowy and dreamlike, the boundary of the little world that I knew. And there, in a cleft between the highest peaks I saw a wondrous thing: for the place at which I was looking seemed to come nearer and nearer to me. I saw the trees, the rocks, the ferns, the white road winding before me; the enfolding hills unclosed like leaves, and in the heart of them I saw a Blue Flower, so bright, so beautiful that my eyes filled with tears as I looked. It was like a face that smiled at me and promised something. Then I heard a call, like the note of a trumpet very far away, calling me to come. And as I listened the flower faded into the dimness of the hills."

"Did you follow it," asked Ruamie, "and did you go away from your home? How could you do that?"

"Yes, Ruamie, when the time came, as soon as I was free, I set out on my journey, and my home is at the end of the journey, wherever that may be."

"And the flower," she asked, "you have seen it again?"

"Once again, when I was a youth, I saw it. After a long voyage upon stormy seas, we came into a quiet haven, and there the friend who was dearest to me said good-bye, for he was going back to his own country and his father's house, but I was still journeying onward. So as I stood at the bow of the ship, sailing out into the wide blue water, far away among the sparkling waves, I saw a little island, with shores of silver sand and slopes of fairest green, and in the middle of the island the Blue Flower was growing, wondrously tall and dazzling, brighter than the sapphire of the sea. Then the call of the distant trumpet came floating across the water, and while it was sounding a shimmer of fog swept over the island and I could see it no more."

"Was it a real island," asked Ruamie. "Did you ever find it?"

"Never, for the ship sailed another way. But once again I saw the flower, three days before I came to Saloma. It was on the edge of the desert, close under the shadow of the great mountains. A vast loneliness was around me; it seemed as if I was the only soul living upon earth, and I longed for the dwellings of men. Then as I woke in the morning I looked up at the dark ridge of the mountains, and there against the brightening blue of the sky I saw the Blue Flower standing up clear and brave. It shone so deep and pure that the sky grew pale around it. Then the echo of the far-off trumpet drifted down the hillsides, and the sun rose, and the flower was melted away in the light. So I rose and traveled on till I came to Saloma."

"And now," said the child, "you are at home with us. Will you not stay for a long, long while? You may find the Blue Flower here. There are many kinds in the fields. I find new ones every day."

"I will stay while I can, Ruamie," I answered, taking her hand in mine as we walked back to the house at nightfall, "but how long that may be I cannot tell. For with you I am at home, yet the place where I must abide is the place where the flower grows, and when the call comes I must follow it."

"Yes," said she, looking at me half in doubt, "I think I understand. But wherever you go I hope you will find the flower at last."

Truthfully there were many things in the city that troubled me and made me restless, in spite of the sweet comfort of Ruamie's friendship and the tranquillity of the life in Saloma. I came to see the meaning of what the old man had said about the shadow that rested upon his thoughts. For there were some in the city who said that the hours of visitation were wasted and that it would be better to employ the time in gathering water from the pools that formed among the mountains in the rainy season or in sinking wells along the edge of the desert. Others had newly come to the city and were teaching that there was no Source and that the story of the poor man who reopened it was a fable and that the hours of visitation were only hours of dreaming. There were many who believed them and many more who said that it did not matter whether their words were true or false and that it was of small concern whether men went to visit the fountain or not, provided only that they worked in the gardens and kept the marble pools and basins in repair and opened new canals through the fields, since there always had been and always would be plenty of water.

As I listened to these sayings it seemed doubtful to me what the final destiny of the city would be. And while this doubt was of grave concern, I heard at midnight the faint calling of the trumpet, sounding along the crest of the mountains. As I went out to look where it came from, I saw, through the glimmering veil of the Milky Way, the shape of a blossom of celestial blue, whose petals seemed to fall and fade as I looked. So I bade farewell to the old man in whose house I had learned to love the hour of visitation and the Source and the name of him who opened it; and I kissed the hands and the brow of the little Ruamie who had entered my heart and journeyed sadly from the land of Koorma into other lands to look for the Blue Flower.

In the Book of the Voyage Without a Harbor is written the record of the ten years that passed before I came back again to the city of Saloma.

It was not easy to find, for I came down through the mountains, and as I looked from a distant shoulder of the hills for the little bay full of greenery, it was not to be seen. There was only a white town shining far off against the brown cliffs, like a flake of formica in a cleft of the rocks. Then I slept that night, full of care, on the hillside and, rising before dawn, came down in the early morning toward the city.

The fields were lying parched and yellow under the sunrise, and great cracks gaped in the earth as if it were thirsty. The trenches and channels were still there, but there was little water in them, and through the ragged fringes of the rusty vineyards I heard, instead of the cheerful songs in the vineyards, the creaking of dry mill wheels and the hoarse throb of the pumps in sunken wells. The girdle of gardens had shrunk like a wreath of withered flowers, and all the bright embroidery of earth was faded to a sullen gray.

At the foot of an ancient, leafless olive tree I saw a group of people kneeling around a newly opened well. I asked a man who was digging beside the dusty path what this might mean. He straightened himself for a moment, wiping the sweat from his brow, and answered sadly, "They are worshiping the wells: how else should they bring water into their fields?" Then he continued furiously to digging again, and I went on into the city.

There was no sound of murmuring streams in the streets, and down the main bed of the river I saw only a few shallow puddles, joined together by a slowly trickling thread. Even these were fenced and guarded so that no one might come near to them, and there were men going among the houses with waterskins on their shoulders, crying, "Water! Water to sell!"

The marble pools in the open square were empty; and at one of them there was a crowd looking at a man who was being beaten with rods. A bystander told me that the officers of the city had ordered him to be punished because he had said that the pools and the basins and the channels were not all of pure marble, without flaw. "For this," he said, "is the evil doctrine that has come in to take away the glory of our city, and because of this the water has failed."

"This is a sad change in the city," I answered, "and no doubt they who have caused it should suffer more than others. But can you tell me at what hour and in what way the people now observe visitation of the Source?"

He looked curiously at me and replied: "I do not understand you. There is no visitation except the inspection of the channels and the wells, which the leaders of the city, whom we call the Princes of Water, carry on daily at every hour. What source is this of which you speak?"

So I went on through the street, where all the passersby seemed in haste and with weary faces, until I came to the house where I had lodged. There was a little basin here against the wall, with a slender stream of water still flowing into it, and a group of children standing near with their pitchers, waiting to fill them.

The door of the house was closed; but, when I knocked, it opened and a young woman came forth. She was pale and sad in appearance, but a light of joy dawned over the snow color of her face, and I knew by the smile in her eyes that it was Ruamie, who had walked with me through the vineyards long ago.

With both hands she welcomed me, saying: "You are expected. Have you found the Blue Flower?"

"Not yet," I answered, "but something drew me back to you. I want to know how it goes with you, and I want to go again with you to visit the Source."

At this her face grew bright, but with a tender half-sad brightness. "The Source!" she said. "Ah, yes, I was sure that you would remember it. And this is the hour of the visitation. Come let us go up together."

Then we went alone through the busy and weary multitudes of the city toward the mountain path. So forsaken was it and so covered with stones and overgrown with wiregrass that I could not have found it except for her guidance. But as we climbed upward the air grew clearer and more sweet, and I questioned her about the things that had come to pass in my absence. I asked her about the kind old man who had taken me into his house when I came as a stranger. She said softly, "He is dead."

"And where are the men and women, his friends, who once thronged this pathway? Are they also dead?"

"They are also dead."

"But where are the younger ones who sang here so gladly as they marched upward? Surely they are living?"

"They have forgotten."

"Where, then, are the young children whose fathers taught them this way and told them to remember it. Have they forgotten?"

"They have forgotten."

"But why have you alone kept the hour of visitation? Why have you not turned back with your companions? How have you walked by yourself day after day?"

She turned to me with a holy regard, and laying her hand gently over mine, she said, "I remember always."

Then I saw a few wildflowers blossoming beside the path.

We drew near to the Source and entered into the chamber cut in the rock. She kneeled and bent over the sleeping spring. She murmured again and again the beautiful name of him who had died to find it. Her voice repeated the song that had once been sung by many voices. Her tears fell softly on the spring, and as they fell it seemed as if the water stirred and rose to meet her bending face, and when she looked up it was as if the dew had fallen on a flower.

We came very slowly down the path along the river Carita and rested often beside it, for surely, I thought, the rising of the spring had sent a little more water down its dry bed, and some of it must flow on to the city. So it was almost evening when we came back to the streets. The people were hurrying to and fro, for it was the day before the choosing of new Princes of Water; and there was much disagreement about them and division over the building of new channels to hold the stores of rain that might fall in the next year. But no one took note of us as we passed by like strangers, and we came unnoticed to the door of the house.

Then a great desire of love and sorrow moved within my breast, and I said to Ruamie, "You are the life of the city, for you alone remember. Its secret is in your heart, and your faithful keeping of the hours of visitation is the only cause why the river has not failed altogether and the curse of desolation returned. Let me stay with you, sweet soul of all the flowers that are dead, and I will cherish you forever. Together we will visit the Source every day; and we shall turn the people, by our lives and by our words, back to that which they have forgotten."

There was a smile in her eyes so deep that its meaning cannot be spoken as she lifted my hand to her lips and answered, "Not so, dear friend, for who can tell whether life or death will come to the city, whether its people will remember at last or whether they will forget forever. Its lot is mine, for I was born here, and here my life is rooted. But you are of the Children of the Unquiet Heart, whose feet can never rest until their task of errors is completed and their lesson of wandering is learned to the end. Until then go forth, and do not forget that I shall remember always."

Behind her quiet voice I heard the silent call that compels us and walked down the street as one walking in a dream. At the place where the path turned aside to the ruined vineyards I looked back. The low sunset made a circle of golden rays about her head and a strange twin blossom of celestial blue seemed to shine in her tranquil eyes.

Since then I do not know what has happened to the city, nor whether it is still called Saloma, or once more Ablis, which is Forsaken. But, if it lives at all,

I know that it is because there is one there who re-members and keeps the hour of visitation and treads the steep way and breathes the beautiful name over the spring, and sometimes I think that long before my seeking and journeying brings me to the Blue Flower it will bloom for Ruamie beside the still waters of the Source.

If as a result of reading this book
you are interested in more information
about how to integrate principles from the Bible
with your life, please write
to the following address:

Northfield Publishing
215 West Locust Street
Chicago, IL 60610

265

Inspirational
vanDyke, Henry
Who Owns the Mountains?